JAPANESE SHORT STORIES FOR INTERMEDIATE LEARNERS

Learn Japanese and Build Your
Vocabulary the Fun and Easy Way

1st Edition

LANGUAGE GURU

Copyright © 2022.

All rights reserved. This book or parts thereof may not be reproduced in any form, stored in any retrieval system, or transmitted in any form by any means—electronic, mechanical, photocopy, recording, or otherwise—without prior written permission of the publisher, except as provided by United States of America copyright law.

ISBN: 978-1-950321-42-1

TABLE OF CONTENTS

Introduction..5
How to Use This Book..8
第 1 章..10
第 2 章..22
第 3 章..32
第 4 章..41
第 5 章..50
第 6 章..60
第 7 章..68
第 8 章..76
第 9 章..86
第 10 章..95
About the Author..104
Did You Enjoy the Read?...106
Answer Key..108

INTRODUCTION

We all know that immersion is the tried and true way to learn a foreign language. After all, it's how we got so good at our first language. The problem is that it's extremely difficult to recreate the same circumstances when we learn a foreign language. We come to rely so much on our native language for everything, and it's hard to make enough time to learn a new one.

We aren't surrounded by the foreign language in our home countries. More often than not, our families can't speak this new language we want to learn. And many of us have stressful jobs or demanding classes that eat away at our limited energy and hours of the day. Immersion can seem like an impossibility.

What we can do, however, is gradually work our way up to immersion no matter where we are in life. And the way we can do this is through extensive reading and listening.

If you have ever taken a foreign language class, chances are you are familiar with intensive reading and listening. In intensive reading and listening, a small amount of text or a short audio recording is broken down line by line, and then, you are drilled on grammar endlessly.

Extensive reading and listening, on the other hand, is quite the opposite. You read a large number of pages or listen to hours and hours of the foreign language without worrying about understanding everything. You rely on context for meaning and try to limit the number of words you need to look up.

If you ask the most successful language learners, it's not intensive but extensive reading and listening that delivers the best results. Simply, volume is much more effective than explicit explanations and rote memorization.

To be able to read like this comfortably, you must practice reading in the foreign language for hours every single day. It takes a massive volume of text before your brain stops intensively reading and shifts into extensive reading.

In the case of Japanese, it does the learner a disservice in the long run if these texts are in romaji (i.e. written using the Latin-Roman alphabet you are reading right now). While it may be incredibly easy to read romaji, a habit of relying on it also widens the gap between you and being able to read Japanese you encounter in the real world. This reliance can even have a negative impact on learning to speak, as romaji can reinforce English speaking patterns and thus ignore consideration for Japanese phonetics.

While the texts in this book feature no romaji, the size of the furigana (the smaller kana that appears above kanji as a reading aid) has been significantly increased as requested by learners. Larger spacing between lines has also been included to make the stories less overwhelming and intimidating to students.

This book hopes to provide a few short stories in Japanese you can use to practice extensive reading. These stories were written and edited by native Japanese speakers from Japan. We hope these short stories help build confidence in your overall reading comprehension skills and encourage you to read more native material. They offer supplementary reading practice with a heavy focus on teaching vocabulary words.

Vocabulary is the number one barrier to entry to extensive reading. Without an active vocabulary base of 10,000 words or more, you'll be stuck constantly looking up words in the dictionary, which will be sure to slow down your reading early on. To speed up

Introduction

the rate at which you read, building and maintaining a vast vocabulary range is absolutely vital. This is why it's so important to invest as much time as possible into immersing yourself in native Japanese every single day. This includes both reading and listening as well as being around native speakers through any and all means possible. Reading manga in Japanese and watching anime without subtitles is highly encouraged.

We hope you enjoy the book and find it useful in growing your Japanese vocabulary and bringing you a few steps closer to extensive reading and fluency!

HOW TO USE THIS BOOK

To simulate extensive reading better, we recommend keeping things simple and using the short stories in the following manner. Read through each story just once and no more. In general, whenever you encounter a word you don't know, first try to guess its meaning using the surrounding context. If its meaning is still unclear and the word is in **bold**, check that chapter's vocabulary list for a simplified definition. If the unknown word is not in bold, a quick online dictionary search may be required.

In our vocabulary lists, we have strived both to include as many potentially new words and phrases as possible but also to keep each list as brief as possible. As a result, each list is quite expansive, but we did leave out several words that can be understood via context as well as the most basic words.

Our recommendation is to read each story silently. While reading aloud can seem beneficial for pronunciation and intonation, it's a practice more aligned with intensive reading. It will further slow down your reading pace and make it considerably more difficult for you to get into extensive reading. If you want to work on pronunciation and intonation, consider practicing these during study and review times rather than reading time. Alternatively, you could also speak to a Japanese tutor or friend to practice what you learned.

After completing the reading for each chapter, test your knowledge of the story by answering the comprehension questions. Check your answers using the answer key located at the end of the book.

How to Use This Book

As a means of review, memorization of any kind is completely unnecessary for language acquisition. The actual language acquisition process occurs subconsciously, and any effort to memorize new vocabulary and grammar structures only stores this information in your short-term memory. Attempting to force new information into your long-term memory only serves to eat up your time and make it that much more frustrating when you can't recall it in the future.

If you wish to review new information that you have learned from the short stories, there are several options that would be wiser. Spaced Repetition Systems (SRS) allow you to cut down on your review time by setting specific intervals in which you are tested on information in order to promote long-term memory storage. Anki and the Goldlist Method are two popular SRS choices that give you the ability to review whatever information you'd like from whatever material you'd like.

Trying to actively review every single new thing you learn, however, will slow you down on your overall path to fluency. While there may be hundreds or even thousands of sentences you want to practice and review, perhaps the best way to go about internalizing it all is to forget it. If it's that important, it will come up through more reading and listening to more Japanese. Languages are more effectively acquired when we allow ourselves to read and listen to them naturally.

And with that, it is time to get started with our main character Makoto and the ten stories about his life. Good luck, reader!

第1章

　ここ数日、マコトは息苦しさを感じていた。30歳という年齢で、このような症状が出るのは少し不自然だ。喫煙者であれば納得がいくかもしれないが、これまで一度もタバコを吸ったことはない。そこで、マコトは医者に診てもらうことにした。

　幸いなことに、その週のうちに病院の予約を取り、診察してもらうことができた。しかし、診察までの待ち時間がとにかく長い。待合室で読むための本を持参していたが、自分の体調を考えると、あまり長い間集中できない。20分もすると、頭が割れるような痛みが襲ってきた。しかし、そんなこともあろうかと市販の鎮痛剤を車に積んでいた。車を往復して、水飲み場の水で薬を流し込んで、ほっと一息ついた。

第1章

　看護婦がマコトを107号室に呼び、簡単な診察をしてもらった。血圧、身長、体重を測り、親族の病歴を聞いてきた。ラッキーなことに、マコトは遺伝性の問題は持っていないようだ。心臓病、ガン、糖尿病、関節炎など、心配するような家族の病歴はない。看護婦が服用している薬についても尋ねてきたが、「薬は飲んでいない」と答えた。

　看護婦は、マコトの情報をカルテに記録した後、「もうすぐ医者が来ます」といって診察室を出て行った。そしてその2分後、ついに医師が目の前に現れた。タカダと名乗る医師は、とても気さくな人だった。二人は呼吸器系の問題について話し合った。胸痛は一日中あるが、動悸はない。咳は少し出るが、喘ぎはない。医師は聴診器をマコトの胸に当て、何度か深呼吸をするように言った。

　かすかにうなずきながら、タカダは最終的な診断を下したようだ。診断内容は喘息だった。子供だけでなく、大人でも喘息になるこ

とはよくあることだという。吸入器を使えばすぐに症状は抑えられるが、一生飲み続けなければならない薬らしい。

先生に渡された処方箋を手に、マコトは吸入器を受け取るために薬局に向かった。薬局の窓口で処方箋のことを尋ねると、しばらく待つように言われ、暇つぶしに店内の棚にあるさまざまな薬を見て回ると、風邪やアレルギー、インフルエンザに効く薬がたくさん並んでいる。便秘や下痢に効く市販薬もある。

そうこうしているうちに薬剤師がマコトの名前を呼んだ、やっと薬を受け取って帰れる。駐車場に停めた車の中で、マコトは1錠飲むと、たちまち気分が良くなった。呼吸が楽になり、胸の痛みも治まった。現代の科学と医学の奇跡には感謝せねばならない。

この経験を経て、マコトは自分の健康や身体がいかに大切なものかを思い知らされた。常に体調が悪いと、生活の質も悪くなる。そのためには、まず食生活から改善しなければならない。

第1章

単語

- 息苦しい（いきぐるしい）――― choking, stuffy, suffocating
- 症状（しょうじょう）――― symptom, condition
- 不自然（ふしぜん）――― unnatural, artificial
- 喫煙者（きつえんしゃ）――― smoker
- 納得がいく（なっとくがいく）――― to accept, to be satisfied with, to make sense
- 吸う（すう）――― to breathe, to smoke, to suck
- ことはない ――― never happens, there is no need to
- 診てもらう（みてもらう）――― to see a doctor
- ことにする ――― to decide to, to make it a rule to
- 幸いなことに（さいわいなことに）――― fortunately, luckily, thankfully
- 予約を取る（よやくをとる）――― to make an appointment
- 診察（しんさつ）――― medical examination
- とにかく ――― anyway, just, anyhow
- 待合室（まちあいしつ）――― waiting room
- ため ――― for, in order to, because of
- 持参（じさん）――― bringing, taking, carrying
- 体調（たいちょう）――― health, physical condition
- 長い間（ながいあいだ）――― long (time), for quite some time
- 集中（しゅうちゅう）――― concentration, focus
- すると ――― then, and, and then

- 痛(いた)み ーーー pain, ache
- 襲(おそ)う ーーー to attack, to strike
- 〜てくる ーーー to do something and come back, to start
- 市販(しはん) ーーー commercial, over-the-counter
- 鎮痛剤(ちんつうざい) ーーー painkiller, pain reliever
- 積(つ)む ーーー to pack, to load, to pile up
- 往復(おうふく) ーーー making a round trip, going and returning
- 水飲(みずの)み場(ば) ーーー water fountain, waterhole
- 流(なが)し込(こ)む ーーー to pour into, to wash down
- ほっと一息(ひといき) ーーー sigh of relief
- 吐(つ)く *(usually written in just kana)* ーーー to breathe out, to vomit
- 看護婦(かんごふ) ーーー (female) nurse
- 号室(ごうしつ) ーーー suffix for room numbers
- 血圧(けつあつ) ーーー blood pressure
- 身長(しんちょう) ーーー height
- 体重(たいじゅう) ーーー (body) weight
- 測(はか)る ーーー to measure, to weigh
- 親族(しんぞく) ーーー relative, family
- 病歴(びょうれき) ーーー medical history
- 遺伝性(いでんせい) ーーー hereditary, inherited, genetic
- 心臓病(しんぞうびょう) ーーー heart disease, heart condition

第1章

- ガン ーーー cancer
- 糖尿病(とうにょうびょう) ーーー diabetes
- 関節炎(かんせつえん) ーーー arthritis
- など ーーー etc., such as, things like
- 服用(ふくよう) ーーー taking medicine
- カルテ ーーー patient's chart, medical record
- 記録(きろく) ーーー record, document
- 医師(いし) ーーー doctor, physician
- 現れる(あらわれる) ーーー to appear, to become visible
- 名乗る(なのる) ーーー to give one's name (as), to call oneself
- 気さく(きさく) ーーー friendly, sociable
- 呼吸器系(こきゅうきけい) ーーー respiratory system
- 胸痛(きょうつう) ーーー chest pain
- 一日中(いちにちじゅう) ーーー all day long, throughout the day
- 動悸(どうき) ーーー palpitation
- 咳(せき) ーーー cough, coughing
- 喘ぎ(あえぎ) ーーー gasping, wheezing
- 聴診器(ちょうしんき) ーーー stethoscope
- 胸(むね) ーーー chest, breast(s)
- 当てる(あてる) ーーー to hit, to put on, to guess
- 深呼吸(しんこきゅう) ーーー deep breath

- かすか ーーー faint, slight

- うなずく ーーー to nod

- 最終的(さいしゅうてき) ーーー final, end

- 診断(しんだん) ーーー diagnosis, diagnostic

- 下(くだ)す ーーー to make a decision, to lower, to do oneself

- 診断内容(しんだんないよう) ーーー diagnosis (contents, details, information)

- 喘息(ぜんそく) ーーー asthma

- だけでなく ーーー not only...but also

- という ーーー named, called, that

- 吸入器(きゅうにゅうき) ーーー inhaler

- 抑(おさ)える ーーー to suppress, to curb

- 一生(いっしょう) ーーー whole life, lifetime

- らしい ーーー seeming, typical of, -ish

- 渡(わた)す ーーー to pass, to give, to carry across

- 処方箋(しょほうせん) ーーー prescription

- 薬局(やっきょく) ーーー pharmacy

- 向(む)かう ーーー to head towards, to face

- 窓口(まどぐち) ーーー counter, window, contact (person)

- しばらく ーーー for a while, for a moment, for the time being

- 暇(ひま)つぶし ーーー killing time, waste of time

- 店内(てんない) ーーー inside of a store

第1章

- 棚(たな) --- shelf, rack
- さまざま --- various
- 見(み)て回(まわ)る --- to look around
- アレルギー --- allergy
- 効(き)く --- to be effective, to work (well)
- 並(なら)ぶ --- to line up, to stand in a line, to match
- 便秘(べんぴ) --- constipation
- 下痢(げり) --- diarrhea
- そうこうしているうちに --- meanwhile, in the meantime
- 薬剤師(やくざいし) --- pharmacist
- 駐車場(ちゅうしゃじょう) --- parking lot
- 1錠(じょう) --- one pill, one tablet
- たちまち --- immediately, quickly, suddenly
- 楽(らく) --- easy, easier, comfortable
- 治(おさ)まる --- to subside
- 現代(げんだい) --- modern, contemporary
- 医学(いがく) --- medicine, medical science
- 奇跡(きせき) --- miracle
- 感謝(かんしゃ) --- thanks, gratitude, appreciation
- ねばならない --- have to do, must do
- 経験(けいけん) --- experience

- 経る（へる）--- to go through, to experience
- 健康（けんこう）--- health, healthy
- 身体（しんたい）--- body, physical
- いかに --- how (much), however (much)
- 思い知る（おもいしる）--- to realize
- 常に（つねに）--- always, constantly
- 質（しつ）--- quality
- そのため --- for that reason
- 食生活（しょくせいかつ）--- eating habits
- 改善（かいぜん）--- improvement

読解問題（どっかいもんだい）

1. マコトはどのような喫煙者（きつえんしゃ）でしたか。
   A) 社交（しゃこう）の場（ば）でのみ喫煙（きつえん）する
   B) 一日（いちにち）に一箱（ひとはこ）
   C) 肺気腫（はいきしゅ）を患（わずら）っていた
   D) 人生（じんせい）で一度（いちど）もタバコを吸（す）ったことがなかった

第1章

2. マコトはどのようにして頭痛を治しましたか？
    A) 医者が治してくれた
    B) 痛み止めを飲んだ
    C) 吸入器を使った
    D) 看護婦が額をマッサージしてくれた

3. 次のうち、重大な病気と見なされないものはどれですか？
    A) 心臓病
    B) 咳
    C) 糖尿病
    D) ガン

4. 医者が人体や動物の体内音を聞くために使う道具は何ですか？
    A) 処方箋
    B) 聴診器
    C) 診断書
    D) 症状

5. 吸入器にはどんな効果がありますか？
    A) 喘息の症状を抑える
    B) 喘息が他の人に広がるのを防ぐ
    C) 喘息がガンにならないようにする
    D) 喘息を完全に治す

English Translation

For the past few days, Makoto has had some difficulty breathing. He was 30 years old, and it was a bit odd for someone his age to have this symptom. Things might make more sense if he was a smoker, but Makoto had never smoked a cigarette in his life. So he decided to go see his doctor about it.

Luckily, he was able to schedule an appointment at the hospital that very week and get himself checked out. Nevertheless, the waiting period before you could be seen by the physician was long. Makoto brought a book to read in the waiting room, but given his condition, he found it hard to focus for very long. After 20 minutes, he started to get a splitting headache. But in anticipation of such a thing, he kept over-the-counter pain relievers in his car. Following a quick trip and back, he washed down the pills with water from the water fountain and breathed a sigh of relief.

The nurse called Makoto into room 107 and performed a basic check-up on him. She measured his blood pressure, height, and weight, and asked about his family's medical history. Luckily, Makoto did not seem to have any hereditary health issues. There was no family history of heart disease, cancer, diabetes, or arthritis to worry about. The nurse also asked about any current drugs he was taking, but he replied, "I don't take any medication."

After the nurse recorded Makoto's information, the nurse said the doctor would be with him shortly and then left the examination room. And just two minutes later, the doctor finally appeared before his eyes. He introduced himself as Dr. Takada and was as friendly as could be. The two discussed Makoto's respiratory issue. Chest pains occurred throughout the day, but there were no heart palpitations. There was a little coughing but no wheezing. The doctor placed his stethoscope on Makoto's chest and asked him to take a couple of deep breaths.

第1章

With a few slight nods, it appeared Dr. Takada had reached a final diagnosis. It was asthma. He said it was common for not just children but adults as well to develop asthma. Using an inhaler would immediately curb his symptoms, but it's a medication he would have to take for the rest of his life.

With his prescription from Dr. Takada, Makoto headed towards the pharmacy to receive his inhaler. When he asked about his prescription at the pharmacy counter, they asked him to wait for a while, so to kill some time, he looked around at the various medicines on the store's shelves, seeing tons of products to treat colds, allergies, and the flu. There were even over-the-counter treatments for constipation and diarrhea.

Meanwhile, the pharmacist called Makoto's name, for finally, he could pick up his prescription and go home. While out in his car in the parking lot, Makoto took one dose and instantly felt better. It became easier to breathe, and his chest pains subsided. He was beyond grateful for the miracle of modern science and medicine.

Throughout this experience, Makoto realized how important his health and body were. If you were in a constant state of bad health, your quality of life would deteriorate. For that reason, his diet must be the first place to start making improvements.

第2章

マコトはダイエットを始めて4週間が経ち、すでに5キロの減量に成功した。新しいダイエット法は非常に厳しいものだが、忠実に守って続けてきたのだ。

朝食は、白いご飯に納豆をのせて食べる。バナナ、味噌汁、わかめなど、おかずも一緒に食べる。そしてもちろん、緑茶も欠かさない。

昼食は、ダイエット法に沿った食事をとりたいので、ヘルシーなお弁当を用意する。おにぎりとともに、枝豆、ミニトマト、ブロッコリー、じゃがいも、たくあん、もやしを食べる。ご飯や芋はカロリーが高いので、少量に抑えている。お弁当でお腹が満たされない時は、果物を追加。果物の中ではブドウがお気に入りだ。

第2章

夕食のメニューは、その日の気分に合わせていくつか選ぶ。ざるそばをつゆとワサビと一緒にすすったり、ネギをのせたうどん、漬物といなりずしでもいい。どれも調理が必要だがそれだけの価値がある。

5週目に入るまで、マコトのダイエットは順調だった。ただし、多くの社会人と同様に、彼もストレスの多い仕事をしているため、毎回の食事を用意する時間が十分にあるとは言えなかった。彼のエネルギー量は下がり始め、一方で食欲と空腹感は急速に高まり始めていた。

やがて、朝食の定番だったご飯と納豆がコンビニの菓子パンに、緑茶は砂糖とミルクで薄めたコーヒーに代わっていった。

昼食のお弁当は、会議で遅くなることが多いことから、ファーストフードに。本来なら昼食と共に水を飲んでいたのだが、今は炭酸飲料がお供だ。

そして、夕食もしばらくすると絶望的な状態になってしまう。仕事で疲れて帰ってくると、料理をする気になれなかったのだ。ピザやアイスクリーム、ラーメン、スナック菓子などの方がずっと楽で、なぜだか不安な気持ちも解消された。

すると数週間後、彼の体重は5キロリバウンドしただけでなく、そこからさらに5キロ増えてしまったのだ！その失敗がマコトの気持ちをさらに萎えさせ、次のダイエットは、もっと厳しく、もっと食べる量を減らそうと心に誓った。

しかし、カロリーの大幅な減少が、エネルギーレベルやジャンクフードへの欲求の大幅な増加を引き起こしていることにマコトは気づいていない。健康的な食べ物をたくさん食べて、ゆっくりとカロリーを減らすことが賢明な方法であることを理解するまで、何度も同じ挑戦をすることになるのだ。

第2章

単語(たんご)

- 経(た)つ ーーー to pass (of time)
- すでに ーーー already, too late
- 減量(げんりょう) ーーー weight loss, reduction
- 成功(せいこう) ーーー success
- 法(ほう) ーーー law, act, method
- 非常(ひじょう)に ーーー very, extremely, quite
- だが ーーー but, however, (and) yet
- 忠実(ちゅうじつ) ーーー faithful, true, loyal
- 守(まも)る ーーー to protect, to defend, to keep (i.e. a promise)
- 朝食(ちょうしょく) ーーー breakfast
- 納豆(なっとう) ーーー natto (fermented soybeans)
- 乗(の)せる ーーー to place on, to pick up, to carry
- 味噌汁(みそしる) ーーー miso soup
- わかめ ーーー wakame (an edible seaweed)
- おかず ーーー side dish
- 緑茶(りょくちゃ) ーーー green tea
- 欠(か)かす ーーー to miss (doing), to fail (to do)
- 昼食(ちゅうしょく) ーーー lunch
- 沿(そ)う ーーー to follow (i.e. a diet), to run along, to be in line with
- 食事(しょくじ)を摂(と)る ーーー to have a meal, to take a meal

Japanese Short Stories for Intermediate Learners

- と共^{とも}に ――― together with, as well as
- 枝豆^{えだまめ} ――― edamame *(green soybeans in pods)*
- たくあん ――― pickled radish
- もやし ――― bean sprouts
- 芋^{いも} ――― potato, sweet potato, taro
- 少量^{しょうりょう} ――― small amount
- 満^みたす ――― to meet (i.e. expectations), to satisfy, to fulfill
- 追加^{ついか} ――― adding, addition, supplement
- ブドウ ――― grape, grapevine
- お気^きに入^いり ――― favorite
- 夕食^{ゆうしょく} ――― dinner
- 合^あわせる ――― to match, to add up, to join together
- ざるそば ――― cold soba noodles served in a basket with sauce
- つゆ ――― (dipping) sauce
- すする ――― to sip, to slurp
- ～たり ――― doing such things like...
- ネギ ――― green onion, scallion
- 漬物^{つけもの} ――― Japanese pickled vegetables
- いなり寿司^{ずし} ――― sushi stuffed in fried tofu
- 調理^{ちょうり} ――― cooking, food preparation
- それだけの価値^{かち}がある ――― it's worth it

第2章

- 順調（じゅんちょう） ーーー doing well, going well
- ただし ーーー however, but
- 社会人（しゃかいじん） ーーー working adult, member of society
- 同様に（どうように） ーーー similarly, likewise, like
- エネルギー ーーー energy
- 量（りょう） ーーー amount, quantity, volume
- 一方で（いっぽうで） ーーー meanwhile, on the one hand, on the other hand
- 食欲（しょくよく） ーーー appetite
- 空腹感（くうふくかん） ーーー feeling hungry
- 急速（きゅうそく） ーーー rapid
- 高まり（たかまり） ーーー rise, surge, swell
- やがて ーーー soon, after a while, eventually
- 定番（ていばん） ーーー standard, staple, classic
- 菓子パン（かしパン） ーーー pastry, sweet bread
- 薄める（うすめる） ーーー to dilute, to water down
- 代わる（かわる） ーーー to replace, to substitute, to take the place of
- 本来（ほんらい） ーーー original(ly), naturally, by nature
- 炭酸飲料（たんさんいんりょう） ーーー soda, carbonated drink
- お供（おとも） ーーー companion, accompanying, attendant
- 絶望的（ぜつぼうてき） ーーー desperate, hopeless
- 状態（じょうたい） ーーー state, situation, condition

- ～てしまう --- to do completely, to do accidentally
- ～気(き)になれない --- don't feel like doing
- スナック菓子(がし) --- snack food
- なぜだか --- somehow, without knowing why
- 不安(ふあん) --- anxiety, uneasiness
- 解消(かいしょう) --- cancellation, resolution
- さらに --- further(more), in addition
- 萎(な)える --- to wither, to lose strength
- 減(へ)らす --- to reduce, to decrease
- 心(こころ)に誓(ちか)う --- to promise, vow, or swear to oneself
- 大幅(おおはば) --- large, substantial
- 減少(げんしょう) --- decrease, decline, reduction
- 欲求(よっきゅう) --- desire
- 増加(ぞうか) --- increase, growth
- 引(ひ)き起(お)こす --- to cause
- 気(き)づく --- to notice, to realize
- 健康的(けんこうてき) --- healthy
- 賢明(けんめい) --- wise
- 方法(ほうほう) --- method, way
- 理解(りかい) --- understanding, comprehension
- 挑戦(ちょうせん) --- challenge

第2章

- ことになる ーーー It has been decided that..., It turns out that...

読解問題(どっかいもんだい)

1. マコトは昼食(ちゅうしょく)にご飯(はん)と芋(いも)をどれだけ食(た)べていましたか？
   A) 全(まった)く食べなかった
   B) 大量(たいりょう)に食(た)べていた
   C) 少量(しょうりょう)に抑(おさ)えていた
   D) 好(す)きなだけ食(た)べていた

2. マコトの好(す)きな夕食(ゆうしょく)は何(なん)でしたか？
   A) ざるそば（つゆとワサビ付(つ)き）
   B) ネギをのせたうどん
   C) いなり寿司(ずし)と漬(つ)け物(もの)
   D) マコトの好物(こうぶつ)が何(なん)であるかは書(か)かれていない

3. ダイエットを始(はじ)めて5週間目(しゅうかんめ)に何(なに)が起(お)こり始(はじ)めましたか？
   A) エネルギー量(りょう)が上昇(じょうしょう)し、食欲(しょくよく)と空腹感(くうふくかん)が急速(きゅうそく)に低下(ていか)し始(はじ)めた
   B) エネルギー量(りょう)は下(さ)がり始(はじ)め、食欲(しょくよく)と空腹感(くうふくかん)は急速(きゅうそく)に上昇(じょうしょう)し始(はじ)めた
   C) エネルギー量(りょう)は変(か)わらず、食欲(しょくよく)と空腹感(くうふくかん)が急速(きゅうそく)に高(たか)まり始(はじ)めた
   D) エネルギー量(りょう)は下(さ)がり始(はじ)めたものの、食欲(しょくよく)と空腹感(くうふくかん)は変(か)わらなかった

Japanese Short Stories for Intermediate Learners

4. ピザ、アイスクリーム、ラーメン、スナック菓子は通常次のうちどれだと考えられていますか？

   A) 健康食品

   B) バランスの取れた朝食

   C) ジャンクフード

   D) 低カロリー食品

5. マコトが90キロでダイエットを始めたとしたら、物語の終わりには何キロになったでしょう？

   A) 85キロ

   B) 90キロ

   C) 95キロ

   D) 100キロ

English Translation

Makoto had been on a diet now for four weeks and had already lost five kilos. His new diet was very strict, but he followed it diligently.

For breakfast, he ate white rice topped with natto. He also had a side dish with his meal, like a banana, miso soup, or wakame. And of course, he never went without his green tea.

For lunch, in order to stick to his meal plan, he prepared a healthy obento. Along with onigiri, he had edamame, mini tomatoes, broccoli, potatoes, pickled radish, and bean sprouts. Rice and potatoes are high in calories, so he kept them to just small portions. If the obento did not fill him up, he had fruit as well. Among fruits, grapes were his favorite.

第2章

For dinner, there were a few options available, depending on what he wanted that night. He could have zarusoba with tsuyu and wasabi, udon noodles topped with green onions, or inarizushi with pickled vegetables. All choices required some cooking, but it was worth it.

All was going pretty well for Makoto until the fifth week started. But like many working adults, he had a stressful job, so you could say there wasn't always enough time to prepare every meal. His energy levels started dropping, while his appetite and hunger rose rapidly.

Soon, his staple breakfast of rice and natto was replaced by pastries from the convenience store, and the green tea was now coffee drowned in milk and sugar.

The obento for lunch turned into fast food since Makoto was often running late for meetings. Originally, he was drinking water with his lunch, but now it was with soda.

And dinner became just hopeless after a while. When Makoto came home exhausted from work, he never felt like cooking. Pizza, ice cream, ramen, and snacks were much easier choices and took his mind off all the anxiety.

Then, several weeks later, not only had he regained all five kilos he had lost, he gained an additional five kilos on top of that! The failure made Makoto feel even worse, so he vowed that for his next diet he would be even more strict and eat even less food.

Nonetheless, he didn't realize that the massive drop in calories was causing a massive dip in his energy levels and cravings for junk food. It would take many attempts before he finally learned that eating lots of healthy foods and slowly cutting down calories would be the wiser move.

第3章

マコトは、もっと自分の身体を大切にしようと、運動を始めることにした。運動はストレス解消になるし、増えた体重も減らすことができる。来週から週5日、ジョギングを始めることに決めた。

初日、彼は出勤前に早起きしてテニスシューズを履き、さっそく走り出す。ストレッチをした後、ジョギングを開始するが、2分もしないうちに息を切らしてしまった。呼吸が荒くなりゼーゼー言っている。わずか5分後には、ジョギングからウォーキングに切り替わってしまった。喘息のせいにするのは簡単だが、彼は単に運動不足なのだと気づいていた。

1日が過ぎ、1週間が過ぎ、数週間が数ヶ月に...時間が経つにつれて、30分ほど走り続けられるようになった。1年後、2年後には、

第3章

マラソン大会に出場できるかもしれないと彼は思ったが、有酸素運動だけでは飽き足らず、次のステップへ移ることにした。

友人であるカズオとマサヒロから、仕事帰りにウエイトトレーニングに誘われ、みんなでジムへ通うことに。週5日、胸、背中、肩、脚、腕と各部位を鍛えることにした。

毎日、激しい運動が必要となったが、運動が終わった時のエンドルフィンは、その甲斐があったと感じさせてくれる。クールダウンには、ランニングマシンで歩いたり、サウナで10分ほど汗を流したりしてリラックスする。

しばらくして、マコトはウェイトリフティングが自分には合っていないと判断した。カズオとマサヒロの競争心が強すぎることから、トレーニングの激しさが楽しさよりも苦痛になってしまったのだ。しかし、ジムでヨガ教室が開かれていることを知ると、マコトは勇気を出して申し込んでみた。

ヨガは、体をほぐし、心を落ち着かせるために、さまざまなストレッチやポーズを行うストレッチのようなものだ。決して楽なレッスンではないので、参加者たちは皆、汗だくになっている。とはいえ、ウェイトリフティングのような激しい運動ではないし、ジョギングよりもずっと楽しくてリラックスできる。

マコトは、毎回のレッスンで爽快な気分になり、また来たいと思うようになった。毎週会うのが楽しみだと思えるような女の子たちとも知り合って、おしゃべりをするようになった。そんな日常も、日課を維持するためのモチベーションとなったのだ。

単語

- 大切にする ーーー to take good care of, to cherish, to value
- 〜し ーーー and, not only … but also, the thing is
- 初日 ーーー first day, day one, opening day
- 出勤 ーーー going to work, being at work
- 履く ーーー to wear or put on lower-body clothing (e.g. shoes)
- さっそく ーーー immediately, right away
- 走り出す ーーー to start running

第3章

- 開始(かいし) ーーー start
- 息(いき)を切(き)らす ーーー to be out of breath
- 荒(あら)い ーーー rough, wild, coarse
- ゼーゼー言(い)う ーーー to wheeze, to gasp for air
- わずか ーーー only, a little, merely
- 切(き)り替(か)わる ーーー to switch, to change completely
- せいにする ーーー to blame
- 単(たん)に ーーー simply, just, merely
- 運動不足(うんどうぶそく) ーーー lack of exercise
- 過(す)ぎる ーーー to pass, to be too much, to be no more than
- につれて ーーー as, with, in proportion to
- ほど ーーー about, as … as *(used in comparisons)*, limit
- ようになる ーーー to reach the point that, to come to
- 大会(たいかい) ーーー tournament, competition, convention
- 出場(しゅつじょう) ーーー entering a competition, appearance, performance
- 有酸素運動(ゆうさんそうんどう) ーーー cardio (workout), aerobic exercise
- 飽(あ)き足(た)らない ーーー not satisfied, not good enough
- ～ず ーーー not
- 移(うつ)る ーーー to move, to shift, to be infected
- 友人(ゆうじん) ーーー friend
- 誘(さそ)う ーーー to invite, to ask, to tempt

- 肩(かた) ーーー shoulder
- 各(かく) ーーー each
- 部位(ぶい) ーーー part (of the body), cut (of meat)
- 鍛(きた)える ーーー to train, to forge, to hone
- 激(はげ)しい ーーー intense, violent, fierce
- となる ーーー to become *(implying a final stage has been reached)*
- エンドルフィン ーーー endorphins
- 甲斐(かい)がある ーーー to be worth it
- 汗(あせ)を流(なが)す ーーー to sweat, to work hard
- しばらくして ーーー after a while, some time later
- 判断(はんだん) ーーー judgment, decision
- 競争心(きょうそうしん) ーーー competitive spirit
- よりも ーーー more than, in comparison to
- 苦痛(くつう) ーーー pain, suffering, agony
- 勇気(ゆうき)を出(だ)す ーーー to be brave, to muster up courage
- 申(もう)し込(こ)む ーーー to apply for, to sign up for, to request
- ほぐす ーーー to loosen (up), to untangle, to relax
- 落(お)ち着(つ)く ーーー to calm (down), to settle (down)
- 行(おこな)う ーーー to perform, to carry out, to do
- 決(けっ)して〜ない ーーー never, by no means
- 参加者(さんかしゃ) ーーー participant

第3章

- 汗(あせ)だく ーーー dripping with sweat, sweaty
- とはいえ ーーー (al)though, having said that, be that as it may be
- 爽快(そうかい) ーーー refreshing, exhilarating
- 知(し)り合(あ)う ーーー to get to know
- おしゃべり ーーー chat, talk, talkative
- 日常(にちじょう) ーーー everyday, ordinary, regular
- 日課(にっか) ーーー daily routine, daily lesson
- 維持(いじ) ーーー maintenance, preservation

読解問題(どっかいもんだい)

1. マコトはどんな靴(くつ)を履(は)いて走(はし)っていましたか？

   A) スパイク

   B) テニスシューズ

   C) ハイヒール

   D) ランニングシューズ

2. マコトがランニングをやめた理由(りゆう)は何(なん)ですか？

   A) 目標(もくひょう)を達成(たっせい)したから
   B) 早起(はやお)きするのが面倒(めんどう)になったから

   C) つまらなかったから
   D) マラソンに参加(さんか)したくなかったから

3. マコト、カズオ、マサヒロの3人は、どんなトレーニングスケジュールで筋トレをしていましたか？

   A) 胸、背中、肩、脚、腕

   B) 胸、背中、ランニング、脚、有酸素運動

   C) 胸、水泳、肩、ランニング、腕

   D) ヨガ、有酸素運動、ジョギング、ウェイトリフティング、スポーツ

4. 3人は運動した後、どのようにリラックスしていたのでしょうか？

   A) 音楽を聴きながらランニングマシンで走った

   B) 10分間のヨガをした

   C) プールで泳いだり、熱いシャワーを浴びたりした

   D) ランニングマシンで10分間歩いたり、サウナで10分間汗を流した

5. マコトはなぜウェイトリフティングをやめたのですか？

   A) 飽きてしまった

   B) 激しすぎて、競争的になりすぎたから

   C) カズオとマサヒロがやめたから

   D) マコトがけがをしたから

第3章

English Translation

In order to take better care of himself, Makoto decided to start exercising. It relieves stress, and it would even help him lose the weight he put on. Starting next week, he would begin running five days a week.

On the first day, he woke up early before work, put on his tennis shoes, and started running right away. After (stopping to do) some stretching, the jogging started, but within two minutes, Makoto was out of breath. His breathing became heavy, and he was wheezing. After just five minutes, the jogging was replaced by walking. It would be easy to blame his asthma, but he realized that he simply lacked exercise.

A day passed, a week passed, and weeks became months. As time went on, Makoto was now able to run continuously for 30 minutes. After a year or two, he may be able to run a marathon, he thought, but he was tired of doing just cardio and decided to move on to the next step.

Makoto's friends Kazuo and Masahiro have invited him to come lift weights after work, so they all decided to go to the gym together. They made it a rule to workout a different part of the body five days a week: chest, back, shoulders, legs, and arms.

Every day, intense exercise became necessary, but the endorphin rush at the end of each workout made it worth it. To cool down, the men relaxed by walking on the treadmills or sweating it out in the sauna for 10 minutes.

After some time, Makoto decided that weightlifting wasn't for him. Kazuo and Masahiro's rivalry was too much, and the intensity of the training had become more painful than fun. But when Makoto found out that a yoga class was being held at the gym, he mustered the courage to sign up.

Yoga is a kind of stretching exercise involving various stretches and poses to relax the body and calm the mind. It was never an easy lesson, and all the participants would be dripping with sweat. Having said that, it was not as intense as weightlifting, and it was much more fun and relaxing than jogging.

Makoto felt refreshed after each class, wanting to come back for more. He also got to know and chat with some of the girls, whom he looked forward to seeing every week. Such was a routine that motivated him to maintain it.

第4章

「クラスの女の子とデートできたらいいなあ…彼女たちと共通の話題で盛り上がりたい」とマコトは思いはじめていた。

彼の趣味には、共通点のあるようなものもあった。テレビを見たり、映画を見たりするのが好きな人は多いだろう。しかしゲーム好きの女の子はいるだろうか？野球やサッカーが好きな子は？政治や歴史の話をする相手がいれば最高なのだが…

ヨガ教室で最初に会ったサチコは、頭がよさそうな人だとすぐ分かった。ノンフィクションではなく、フィクション物をよく読む人だ。文学が好きで、今読んでいる小説について何時間でも話すことができた。

他にも愛犬の世話や散歩も欠かさずキッチリしている。たまに、ワインを飲みながらホラー映画を見ることもあるらしい。

次にマサコという名の女性と仲良くなったが、彼女はかなり忙しいらしく、話す時間があまりないようだ。後で知ったことだが、彼女はボディービルの選手で、コーチもしているらしい。クライアントとのアポイントメントがなくても、自分のビジネスを拡大させることで精一杯だったのだ。マサコは、ソーシャルメディアに多くのフォロワーを持ち、Tシャツ、スウェットシャツ、帽子、アクセサリーを販売するアパレルブランドを立ち上げていた。仕事中毒と言えるかもしれないが、大きな成功を収めていることは認めざるを得ない。

最後に出会った女性は、少し社交的な性格のカツミだ。たくさんの友人と話し、一緒に過ごす仲間の繋がりをもっていた。外向的であることは会ってすぐに分かった。メールをしていないときは、友人と外出し、お酒を飲んだりクラブに行ったりしているらしい。家にいるときは、マンガを読んだり、テレビゲームをしたりするのが好きなのだそう。

第4章

マコトは、カツミに**一目**ぼれしていた。**今**やっているゲームや**今後発売**されるゲームについて、**一緒**に**オタク**になれる**相手**がやっと**見**つかったからだ。しかし、二人の性格は**あまりに違い過**ぎたため、**相性**がいいとは**言**えない。**お互**いの**趣味以外**の**話**は**一切**できない。

マサコはあまり**話**す**時間**がなかったが、サチコは**喜**んで**一緒**に**時間を過**ごしてくれた。マコトは**彼女が好**きな**本の話を聞**き、オーディオブックで**おすすめの本を読**んでみるように**説得**されたこともあった。サチコはスポーツや**歴史**にはあまり**興味**がなかったが、マコトが**興味**のある**テーマ**について**話**すときでも、**彼**の**情熱**とエネルギーに**惹**きつけられたようだ。そして、**二人**は**互**いに**惹**かれあい、**交際**を**始**めることになる。

単語

- **共通** ――― common, shared
- **話題** ――― topic, subject, highly discussed issue
- **盛り上がる** ――― to excite, to get excited, to swell
- **共通点** ――― something in common, point in common

- <ruby>政治<rt>せいじ</rt></ruby> ――― politics, government
- <ruby>相手<rt>あいて</rt></ruby> ――― partner, opponent, other party
- <ruby>最高<rt>さいこう</rt></ruby> ――― highest, supreme, best
- <ruby>文学<rt>ぶんがく</rt></ruby> ――― literature
- <ruby>小説<rt>しょうせつ</rt></ruby> ――― novel, story
- <ruby>何時間<rt>なんじかん</rt></ruby> ――― how many times, for hours
- <ruby>他<rt>ほか</rt></ruby>にも ――― in addition, furthermore, even more
- <ruby>愛犬<rt>あいけん</rt></ruby> ――― pet dog, beloved dog
- <ruby>世話<rt>せわ</rt></ruby> ――― care, looking after
- キッチリ ――― exactly, tightly, strictly
- たまに ――― sometimes, occasionally
- <ruby>名<rt>な</rt></ruby> ――― name, title
- <ruby>女性<rt>じょせい</rt></ruby> ――― woman, female
- <ruby>仲良<rt>なかよ</rt></ruby>く ――― getting along well, on good terms with, friendly
- かなり ――― quite, pretty, fairly
- ボディービル ――― bodybuilding
- <ruby>選手<rt>せんしゅ</rt></ruby> ――― player (sports), athlete
- <ruby>拡大<rt>かくだい</rt></ruby> ――― expansion, magnification, enlargement
- <ruby>精一杯<rt>せいいっぱい</rt></ruby> ――― the best one can do, to the best of one's ability
- <ruby>販売<rt>はんばい</rt></ruby> ――― sales, selling, marketing
- アパレルブランド ――― clothing brand, apparel brand

第4章

- 立(た)ち上(あ)げる ーーー to launch, to start (up), to boot up a computer
- 仕事中毒(しごとちゅうどく) ーーー workaholism
- 成功(せいこう)を収(おさ)める ーーー to achieve success, to be successful
- 認(みと)める ーーー to acknowledge, to recognize, to admit
- ～ざるを得(え)ない ーーー cannot help but do, no choice but to
- 社交的(しゃこうてき) ーーー sociable, outgoing
- 性格(せいかく) ーーー character, personality, nature
- 仲間(なかま) ーーー buddy, homie, (social) circle
- 繋(つな)がり ーーー connection, link, relationship
- 外向的(がいこうてき) ーーー outgoing, extroverted
- メール ーーー email, text, message
- 外出(がいしゅつ) ーーー going out *(of one's house or office)*
- 一目(ひとめ)ぼれ ーーー love at first sight, a crush on someone
- 今後(こんご) ーーー future, upcoming, from now on
- 発売(はつばい) ーーー launching *(a product)*, releasing *(for sale)*
- オタク ーーー otaku, nerd, geek
- あまりに ーーー too (much)
- 違(ちが)い ーーー difference
- 相性(あいしょう) ーーー compatibility, match, chemistry *(between people)*
- お互(たが)い ーーー each other, one another, mutual
- 以外(いがい) ーーー other than, except

- 一切(いっさい) --- all, everything, completely
- 喜ぶ(よろこ) --- to be pleased, to be glad, to be delighted
- おすすめ --- recommendation
- 説得(せっとく) --- persuasion
- テーマ --- theme, topic, subject
- 情熱(じょうねつ) --- passion, enthusiasm
- 惹(ひ)きつける --- to attract, to charm, to entice
- 惹(ひ)かれ会(あ)う --- to be attracted to each other
- 交際(こうさい) --- association, friendship, dating

読解問題(どっかいもんだい)

1. 誰(だれ)かと共通点(きょうつうてん)がある場合(ばあい)、次(つぎ)のうちどの記述(きじゅつ)が正(ただ)しいですか？
    A) お互(たが)いのことが好(す)き
    B) お互(たが)いに恋(こい)をしている
    C) お互(たが)いに好(す)きではない
    D) お互(たが)いに興味(きょうみ)のある共通(きょうつう)の趣味(しゅみ)を持(も)っている

第4章

2. 次のうち政治、歴史、行政は一般的にどのようなものであると考えられていますか？

   A) フィクション

   B) ノンフィクション

   C) 文学

   D) 上記すべて

3. マサコは女性ボディビル選手・コーチだけでなく次のうちどんな人でしたか？

   A) 個人事業主

   B) アルコール依存症

   C) ヨガインストラクター

   D) 人付き合いのいい人

4. 次のうち、外向的な性格を最もよく表しているのはどれでしょう？

   A) 声が大きくてうるさい人

   B) 大胆な人

   C) おしゃべりな人

   D) 恥ずかしがり屋で控えめな人

5. 最終的に一番相性が良かったカップルは次のうちどれですか？

   A) マコトとカツミ

   B) マコトとマサコ

   C) マコトとサチコ

   D) マコトとヨガインストラクター

English Translation

"I wish I could date those girls from class...I want to find something in common with them and make a connection *(lit. get excited)*", Makoto thought.

His hobbies were somewhat relatable. Everybody likes watching TV and movies. But was there a girl who liked video games? How about a girl who liked professional baseball and soccer? It would be amazing if he had someone to talk to about politics and history.

The first girl he met from yoga class was Sachiko, who seemed really smart right away. She was a big reader of fiction but not non-fiction. She liked literature and could talk for hours about the novel she was currently reading. Besides that, she was very diligent about taking care of her dog and taking him for long walks. And occasionally, she would watch horror movies while drinking wine.

Next, Masako was the second girl he got to know, although she was very busy and didn't have a lot of time to talk. Makoto later learned that she was a bodybuilding athlete and coach. If she didn't have an appointment with a client, she was doing her best to expand her business. Masako had a big social media following and had launched a clothing brand that sold T-shirts, sweatshirts, hats, and accessories. You could say she was a workaholic, but you had to admit she was very successful.

第4章

  The last girl Makoto met was Katsumi, who had a bit of an outgoing personality. She had a large social circle of friends to talk to and hang out with. You immediately knew from meeting her that she was an extrovert. When she wasn't texting, she was out with friends, drinking and clubbing. When she did decide to stay home, Katsumi liked to read manga and play video games.

  Makoto had a crush on Katsumi. He had finally found someone he could nerd out with about current and upcoming games. Their personalities, however, were too different to say they had any chemistry. They couldn't talk about anything outside of their mutual hobby.

  Masako never really had much time to talk, but Sachiko was happy to spend some time with him. Makoto listened to her talk about the books she liked and was even persuaded to try reading a book she recommended via audiobooks. Sachiko wasn't really interested in sports or history, but she was attracted to the passion and energy Makoto had when he spoke about subjects he cared about. And so they became mutually interested in one another and started dating.

第5章

　マコトのプライベートは花盛りだが、職場での生活は正反対であった。保険会社の事務局で給料は良いが、仕事量は半端ではない。

　毎朝、仕事のメールをチェックすると、すぐに対応しなければならない依頼が50件ほど入っている。昼までに処理しないと、予定より遅れてしまい残業は確定。しかも、それを上司が見ているとなればなおさらだ。

　マコトの上司は、社員全員に厳しく接する人物だ。ひとつのミスが、会社に大きな損害を与えることになる。失敗があれば、社員だけでなく上司も厳しい処分を受けることになるのだ。

　保険というのはなかなか難しい商売である。メンタルが弱い者には向かない。会議、書類、規則など、すべてが最重要事項であり、

第5章

何か見逃したり、忘れたりすることは許されない。それが原因でクビになることだってあるのだ。

「どうやって定年まで生きていけばいいのだろう?」マコトは、少なくとも週に一度はこう自問自答する。むしろ週に一度であればラッキーな方で、実際は同じようなことを頻繁に思っている。ストレスと不安で、もう限界だ。精神を崩す一歩手前まで来ていた。

もし別の大学の学位を選んでいたらどんな人生になっていたのだろう?もし、コンピューターサイエンスに進んでいたら?プログラミングならもっと楽しめただろうか?大学の野球部でプレーしながら、もっと自分を追い込んでいたらどうだろう?プロ野球選手になれただろうか?もし、ゲームタレントとして活躍し、プロゲーマーになっていたら?夢のような話だ。

しかし、残念ながらマコトの人生はそうならなかった。嫌な仕事から抜け出せないかもしれないが、少なくとも「変わりたい」という願望は持っている。多くの同僚は、そのような気持ちすら持っていない。う

つ病や不安神経症の人が多い職場だが、中には冗談を言い合って場を和ませてくれる職場仲間もいる。そのおかげで、毎日を過ごすのが少し楽になった。それが何よりの違いだ。

しかし、中には人生の厳しさに打ちのめされ、抜け殻のようになってしまったような人もいる。その人たちの存在は、マコトにとって上司のどんな叱咤よりも恐怖になっていた。

しかし、いつになったら状況は変わるのだろうか？どう変わるのか？ただひとつ確かなことは、何かを変えなければならないということだ。

単語

- プライベート ――― private, private life, privacy
- 花盛り ――― in full bloom, at its best, in its heyday
- 職場 ――― workplace, office
- 正反対 ――― the exact opposite (of)
- 保険会社 ――― insurance company
- 事務局 ――― (administrative) office

第5章

- <ruby>給料<rt>きゅうりょう</rt></ruby> ーーー pay, salary, wages
- <ruby>半端<rt>はんぱ</rt></ruby>ではない ーーー far above average, staggering, incredible
- <ruby>対応<rt>たいおう</rt></ruby> ーーー correspondence, dealing with, compatibility *(tech)*
- <ruby>依頼<rt>いらい</rt></ruby> ーーー request, dependence
- <ruby>件<rt>けん</rt></ruby> ーーー matter, case, counter for messages or accounts
- <ruby>処理<rt>しょり</rt></ruby> ーーー processing, dealing with, treatment
- <ruby>残業<rt>ざんぎょう</rt></ruby> ーーー overtime *(work)*
- <ruby>確定<rt>かくてい</rt></ruby> ーーー decision, settlement, confirmation
- しかも ーーー moreover, furthermore, and yet
- <ruby>上司<rt>じょうし</rt></ruby> ーーー (one's) boss
- となれば ーーー when it comes to, if … happens
- なおさら ーーー all the more, especially, much less
- <ruby>社員<rt>しゃいん</rt></ruby> ーーー employee, staff member, shareholder *(legal context)*
- <ruby>全員<rt>ぜんいん</rt></ruby> ーーー all members, everyone
- <ruby>接<rt>せっ</rt></ruby>する ーーー to come in contact with, to be close, to attend to
- <ruby>人物<rt>じんぶつ</rt></ruby> ーーー person, figure, character
- ミス ーーー mistake, error
- <ruby>損害<rt>そんがい</rt></ruby>を<ruby>与<rt>あた</rt></ruby>える ーーー to damage, to harm
- <ruby>処分<rt>しょぶん</rt></ruby> ーーー disposal, punishment
- というのは ーーー because, the meaning of, as for
- なかなか ーーー quite, pretty, rather

- <ruby>商売<rt>しょうばい</rt></ruby> ――― business, trade, commerce
- メンタル ――― mental, mentality, mental health
- <ruby>弱<rt>よわ</rt></ruby>い<ruby>者<rt>もの</rt></ruby> ――― weakling, the weak
- <ruby>向<rt>む</rt></ruby>く ――― to turn (to/towards), to face, to be suitable for
- <ruby>書類<rt>しょるい</rt></ruby> ――― document, paperwork, papers
- <ruby>規則<rt>きそく</rt></ruby> ――― rule, regulation
- <ruby>最重要<rt>さいじゅうよう</rt></ruby> ――― most important, top priority, key
- <ruby>事項<rt>じこう</rt></ruby> ――― matters, items
- <ruby>見逃<rt>みのが</rt></ruby>す ――― to miss, to overlook, to pass up
- <ruby>許<rt>ゆる</rt></ruby>す ――― to permit, to allow, to forgive
- <ruby>原因<rt>げんいん</rt></ruby> ――― cause, source, origin
- <ruby>首<rt>くび</rt></ruby>になる ――― to be fired
- <ruby>定年<rt>ていねん</rt></ruby> ――― retirement age
- <ruby>少<rt>すく</rt></ruby>なくとも ――― at least
- <ruby>自問自答<rt>じもんじとう</rt></ruby> ――― wondering or talking to oneself
- むしろ ――― rather, instead, but
- <ruby>実際<rt>じっさい</rt></ruby>は ――― actually, in fact, fact is
- <ruby>頻繁<rt>ひんぱん</rt></ruby> ――― frequent(ly)
- <ruby>限界<rt>げんかい</rt></ruby> ――― limit, limitation
- <ruby>精神<rt>せいしん</rt></ruby> ――― mind, spirit
- <ruby>崩<rt>くず</rt></ruby>す ――― to destroy, to demolish, to break

第5章

- 一歩手前（いっぽてまえ） ーーー on the brink, one step short of
- 学位（がくい） ーーー degree, diploma
- 人生（じんせい） ーーー (human) life, one's life
- 楽しむ（たのしむ） ーーー to enjoy (oneself), to have fun
- 野球部（やきゅうぶ） ーーー baseball team, baseball club
- 追い込む（おいこむ） ーーー to herd, to corner, to drive
- タレント ーーー entertainer, talent, personality
- として ーーー as *(i.e. in the role of)*
- 活躍（かつやく） ーーー activity, work, playing an active role
- 残念ながら（ざんねんながら） ーーー unfortunately
- 抜け出す（ぬけだす） ーーー to slip out of, to break free, to lose one's hair
- 願望（がんぼう） ーーー desire, wish
- 同僚（どうりょう） ーーー co-worker

- すら ーーー even
- うつ病（うつびょう） ーーー depression
- 不安神経症（ふあんしんけいしょう） ーーー anxiety disorder
- 冗談（じょうだん） ーーー joke
- 言い合う（いいあう） ーーー to say to each other, to tell jokes etc., to quarrel
- 和む（なごむ） ーーー to calm down, to comfort

- おかげで ーーー thanks to
- 何より（なにより） ーーー more than anything, above all, what matters most

Japanese Short Stories for Intermediate Learners

- 打ちのめす ーーー to beat someone up (physically or emotionally)
- 抜け殻 ーーー empty shell, husk
- 存在 ーーー existence, presence

- にとって ーーー for, to, concerning
- 叱咤 ーーー scolding, reprimanding, encouraging
- 恐怖 ーーー fear, terror

- いつになったら ーーー when, how soon
- 状況 ーーー the situation, state, circumstances

- ただ ーーー ordinary, free, merely
- 確か ーーー certain(ly), reliable, if I remember correctly

- ということだ ーーー I heard that, it means that, it appears that

読解問題

1. もしマコトが昼までにメールを返信できなかったらどうなりますか?
   A) クビになり、すぐに家に帰される
   B) 早く帰ってパソコンでゲームをするようになる
   C) 今後5年間は昇進できない
   D) 予定より遅れてしまい、残業になる可能性が高い

第5章

2. 会社でミスをした場合、誰が処分を受ける可能性がありますか？

   A) 従業員

   B) 上司

   C) 従業員と上司

   D) マコトのみ

3. マコトは生涯を通じて複数の進路を考えていましたが、その中に入っていなかったものはどれですか？

   A) 高校の教師

   B) ゲームタレント

   C) プロ野球選手

   D) コンピュータープログラマー

4. 同僚とは、別の言葉で何と言いますか？

   A) 上司

   B) 友達

   C) マネージャー

   D) 職場仲間

5. 人生の厳しさに打ちのめされている人はどんな症状に悩まされますか？

A) 胃の不調
B) うつや不安
C) 夢が叶う
D) 気分がよくなる

English Translation

While Makoto's private life was blooming, his life at work was the exact opposite. He worked at the administrative office for an insurance company, where the pay was good, but the workload was overwhelming.

 Each morning, he checked his work email and found around 50 new requests that had to be immediately dealt with. If he didn't process them by lunch, he would get caught behind schedule and have to work overtime. Furthermore, if his boss saw this, things would be even worse.

 Makoto's boss was a strict man with all the employees. One mistake and it could cost the company greatly. If there were such a blunder, not only would the employee but the boss too would be subjected to disciplinary action.

 Insurance is a very difficult business. It is not for the weak. Meetings, documents, and regulations are all of the utmost importance, and you cannot miss or forget anything. You could be fired for it!

 "How am I going to make it to retirement?" Makoto asked himself at least once a week. Rather, he was lucky if this question only came up once that week, but in reality, he regularly thought

第5章

about it. His stress and anxiety were at their limits. He was one step away from a mental breakdown.

What would life have been like if he had chosen a different college degree? What if he went into computer science? Would he have enjoyed programming more? What if he pushed himself harder while playing for the college baseball team? Would he have become a professional player? What if he was a gaming personality and became a pro gamer? It would have been a dream come true.

But, unfortunately, Makoto's life didn't turn out that way. He might have been stuck with a job he hated, but at least he had the desire to change. Many of his co-workers did not even have that feeling. There were many people with depression and anxiety in his workplace, but some of his colleagues told jokes and made the workplace more comforting. Thanks to them, it was just a little easier to get through each day. That made all the difference.

There were others, though, who seemed to be beaten down by the harshness of life and were now just empty shells. The mere existence of those people scared Makoto more than any boss ever had.

But when would things change? How would they change? The only thing that was certain was that something must change.

第6章

マコトは、溜まったストレスや不安を解消するために、久々に自然散策に出かけた。1日、2日山で過ごすと、精神的に楽になると聞いたからだ。隔離された空間は、心にデトックスとリフレッシュに効く時間と空間を与えてくれるだろう。他にいる存在と言えば動物だけである。

彼の家は集合住宅の中にあるので、たまにリスを見かける程度で、野生動物を見る機会はほとんどない。たぬきやフクロウなどを見ることはない。室内で過ごすことが多いので、見る生物といったら蚊やゴキブリが多い。ゴキブリは特に好きではない。

山へ行くまでにそれほど時間はかからなかった。駐車場に車を停め、車を降りると、すぐに野原で草を食む数頭の鹿が見える。ゆっくりと草を食べながら尻尾を振っている。挨拶をしようと思っ

第6章

て慎重に近づいたが、20メートルくらいまで近づいたところで、鹿は逃げて行ってしまった。

マコトはどこから散策をはじめるべきか分からなかったが、森の隙間に向かって歩いている他の散策者を見かけると、その疑問は解けた。この森はなんと美しいのだろう。常緑樹と太陽の光が、息を呑むような美しい風景を作り出している。湖が自然の広大さをさらに際立たせ、マコトは心の奥底から自分自身の小ささを感じた。

森の茂みも虫も鳥も、すべて生命が宿っている。平和な調和を感じることができた。もちろん、山の上には熊やヤマネコもいるが、彼らもまた、森の中のすべての生命をつなぐ生態系の一部である。湖畔のカエルも、ダムをつくるビーバーと同じように生きている。違う生き物かもしれないが、同じ世界の小さな一部でしかないのである。宇宙に散らばる同じ化学元素でできているのだ。

太陽が沈むと、森の中にいるのは危険だ。夜になると現れる外敵を避けるために、マコトは車まで素早く歩いた。車の中で、次に来

れるのはいつになるのだろうと考えていた。次回は必ず、サチコと一緒に来よう。

単語

- 溜まる --- to collect, to accumulate, to pile up
- 久々 --- long time, long ago
- 自然散策 --- nature walk
- 精神的 --- mental, emotional
- 隔離 --- isolation, quarantine
- 空間 --- space, room
- デトックス --- detox
- 与える --- to give, to provide, to cause
- 集合住宅 --- apartment building, housing complex
- リス --- squirrel
- 見かける --- to (happen to) see, to catch sight of, to notice
- 程度 --- degree, extent, standard
- 野生動物 --- wild animal, wildlife
- 機会 --- opportunity, chance, occasion
- ほとんどない --- almost no, very little, hardly any
- たぬき --- tanuki, raccoon dog
- フクロウ --- owl

第6章

- 室内（しつない） ーーー indoor, inside the room
- 生物（せいぶつ） ーーー living creature, life, organism
- 蚊（か） ーーー mosquito
- ゴキブリ ーーー cockroach
- それほど ーーー that much, all that, so
- 野原（のはら） ーーー field
- 食む（はむ） ーーー to graze, to eat (grass, hay, or feed)
- 数頭（すうとう） ーーー head count, number of animals
- 鹿（しか） ーーー deer
- 尻尾を振る（しっぽをふる） ーーー to wag one's tail, to flatter, to butter up
- 挨拶（あいさつ） ーーー greeting, saying hello, speech
- 慎重（しんちょう） ーーー careful, cautious
- 近づく（ちかづく） ーーー to approach, to get closer
- くらい ーーー about, around, enough
- ~た + ところで ーーー just when, since, even if
- べき ーーー should, must, have to
- 隙間（すきま） ーーー gap, opening, crack
- 散策者（さんさくしゃ） ーーー walker
- 疑問（ぎもん） ーーー doubt, question
- 解ける（とける） ーーー to be solved, to unravel, to melt
- なんと ーーー what, how, what (a)...!

- 常緑樹（じょうりょくじゅ）--- evergreen tree
- 息を呑むよう（いきをのむよう）--- breathtaking
- 風景（ふうけい）--- scenery, landscape, scene
- 作り出す（つくりだす）--- to create, to produce, to build
- 広大（こうだい）--- vast, extensive, huge
- 際立つ（きわだつ）--- to stand out, to be conspicuous
- 奥底（おくそこ）--- depths, deep place, the bottom
- 自分自身（じぶんじしん）--- oneself
- 茂み（しげみ）--- bush, thicket
- 生命（せいめい）--- life, career, soul
- 宿る（やどる）--- to dwell, to stay at, to lodge at
- 平和（へいわ）--- peace, peaceful(ly)
- 調和（ちょうわ）--- harmony
- ヤマネコ --- wildcat, lynx
- つなぐ --- to connect, to tie, to maintain
- 生態系（せいたいけい）--- ecosystem
- 湖畔（こはん）--- lakeshore
- しかない --- no choice but, nothing but
- 散らばる（ちらばる）--- to be scattered about, to scatter
- 化学元素（かがくげんそ）--- chemical element
- 沈む（しずむ）--- to sink, to set *(e.g. the sun)*, to feel depressed

第6章

- 外敵(がいてき) ーーー foreign enemy, outside invader, predator
- 避ける(さ) ーーー to avoid, to evade, to avert
- 素早い(すばや) ーーー quick, swift, nimble

読解問題(どっかいもんだい)

1. マコトはどこへ自然観察(しぜんかんさつ)に行(い)きましたか？

   A) 山(やま)の頂上(ちょうじょう)
   B) 山(やま)の手線(てせん)
   C) 山(やま)の外(そと)
   D) 山(やま)の中(なか)

2. マコトが住(す)んでいるアパートの周(まわ)りで見(み)かけなかった野生動物(やせいどうぶつ)はどれでしょう？

   A) リス
   B) 熊(くま)
   C) 蚊(か)
   D) ゴキブリ

3. 鹿(しか)は広々(ひろびろ)とした野原(のはら)で何(なに)をしていましたか？

   A) 目(め)を丸(まる)くしていた
   B) 放牧(ほうぼく)
   C) 銃(じゅう)を撃(う)つ
   D) 他(ほか)の動物(どうぶつ)の狩(か)り

4. <ruby>森<rt>もり</rt></ruby>を<ruby>見<rt>み</rt></ruby>て、マコトはどんな<ruby>気持<rt>きも</rt></ruby>ちになりましたか？

   A) あまりにも<ruby>広大<rt>こうだい</rt></ruby>なので、<ruby>自分自身<rt>じぶんじしん</rt></ruby>の<ruby>小<rt>ちい</rt></ruby>ささを<ruby>感<rt>かん</rt></ruby>じた
   B) <ruby>開放的<rt>かいほうてき</rt></ruby>な<ruby>雰囲気<rt>ふんいき</rt></ruby>が<ruby>疲<rt>つか</rt></ruby>れを<ruby>感<rt>かん</rt></ruby>じさせた
   C) <ruby>漠然<rt>ばくぜん</rt></ruby>としていて<ruby>不安<rt>ふあん</rt></ruby>になった
   D) <ruby>狭<rt>せま</rt></ruby>かったので<ruby>自分自身<rt>じぶんじしん</rt></ruby>の<ruby>大<rt>おお</rt></ruby>きさを<ruby>感<rt>かん</rt></ruby>じた

5. マコトの<ruby>話<rt>はなし</rt></ruby>によれば、<ruby>森<rt>もり</rt></ruby>の<ruby>中<rt>なか</rt></ruby>ですべての<ruby>生命<rt>せいめい</rt></ruby>はどのようにつながっていたでしょうか？

   A) ブルドーザーで<ruby>壊<rt>こわ</rt></ruby>されつつある
   B) <ruby>狩猟<rt>しゅりょう</rt></ruby>の<ruby>対象<rt>たいしょう</rt></ruby>になっていた
   C) ひとつの<ruby>生態系<rt>せいたいけい</rt></ruby>として<ruby>平和<rt>へいわ</rt></ruby>に<ruby>調和<rt>ちょうわ</rt></ruby>していた
   D) ストレスや<ruby>不安<rt>ふあん</rt></ruby>を<ruby>解消<rt>かいしょう</rt></ruby>するのに<ruby>適<rt>てき</rt></ruby>していた

English Translation

To relieve some of the stress and anxiety he had been accumulating, Makoto set off on a nature walk for the first time in a long time. He heard that spending a day or two in the mountains would improve his mental health. The isolation would give his mind time and space to detox and refresh. It would be just him and the animals.

His house was inside an apartment complex, so he hardly saw any wildlife besides the occasional squirrel. And he never saw any tanukis or owls. Because he spent most of his time indoors, the creatures he saw the most were mosquitoes and cockroaches. He particularly did not like cockroaches.

It didn't take too long to reach the mountains. Immediately after pulling into the parking lot and exiting his car, he saw a few deer grazing in the field. They were slowly feeding on the grass and

第6章

wagging their tails. He carefully approached them to try to say hello, but when he was about 20 meters from them, the deer ran away.

Makoto was unsure where to begin hiking, but his question was answered when he saw some other walkers strolling towards an opening in the forest. And what a beautiful forest it was! The evergreen trees and sun's rays made for some breathtaking scenery. The lake made the vastness of nature stand out further, and from deep within, Makoto felt how small he was.

The bushes, insects, and birds of the forest all had life in them. A peaceful harmony could be felt. Sure, there were also bears and wildcats up in the mountains, but they too were part of the ecosystem that connected all life in the forest. The frogs on the lakeshore live just like the beavers building dams. They may be different creatures, but they were both just small parts of the same world. They were made from the same chemical elements scattered throughout the universe.

With the sun setting, it became dangerous to stay in the forest. Makoto walked quickly back to his car to avoid predators who came out at night. While in his car, he wondered about the next time he would be able to come back. There would definitely be a next time, and it would definitely have to be with Sachiko.

第7章

　その日、サチコとの大事なデートの前に、マコトはいくつかの用事を済ませておいた。まず、銀行に行って現金を下ろしておかなければならない。銀行へ行く途中、行きつけのコーヒーショップでカフェインを補給して1日をスタートさせる。

　次に、郵便局へ行き、遅れていた郵便物を投函する。そして、デパートに行ってデートに着ていく新しい服を探した。洋服屋を2軒はしごし、美容院で髪を切る余裕もあった。

　午後2時、マコトはサチコと合流し、街を散策することになった。まずは公園を散歩して、お互いの近況を報告し合う。公園の中には大きな広場があり、ロックバンドの小さなコンサートが開かれていた。数曲聴いた後、二人は公園を出て、近くの遊園地へと車を走らせた。

第7章

遊園地は大きな事故があったらしく、閉鎖されていたので二人は映画館に行くことにした。幸いその週はホラー映画が上映されているらしい。映画が上映されるまで1時間の待ち時間があったので、近くのメキシコ料理店で早めに夕食をとり、映画館に戻った。ホラー映画は鳥肌が立つような恐怖を味わうことができたので満足だ。

夜は更け、あまり遅くまで繁華街で遊びたくないという気持ちはあったが、スマートフォンで検索して見つけたユニークなバーで一杯やろうということになる。中世の城をテーマにしたバーで、旗や鎧兜、玉座のような椅子が飾られていた。二人の会話は弾み、さらに酒が進む。

二人とも酔っぱらってしまい、帰りが心配になるほどだった。クラブに行く気分ではないので、2時間後に酔いを覚ましてから家に帰ることにした。タクシーに乗ると高くつくし、そもそもそんなに待つほどでもない。時間をつぶすために遊歩道を歩き、コンビニに寄って軽食をとった。

Japanese Short Stories for Intermediate Learners

マコトとサチコはお互^{たが}いにデートを楽^{たの}しみ、思^{おも}ったより早^{はや}く時間^{じかん}が過^すぎてしまったが、そろそろ別^{わか}れの時間^{じかん}だ。短^{みじか}いキスを交^かわして、二人^{ふたり}は帰路^{きろ}についた。

単語^{たんご}

- 用事^{ようじ} ーーー errand, things to do, business
- 済^すませる ーーー to finish, to get through with, to let end
- 〜ておく ーーー to do in advance
- 現金^{げんきん}を下ろす ーーー to withdraw cash
- 途中^{とちゅう} ーーー on the way, in the middle of, halfway
- 行^いきつけ ーーー regular, favorite, preferred
- カフェイン ーーー caffeine
- 補給^{ほきゅう} ーーー supply, replenishment, refueling
- 郵便物^{ゆうびんぶつ} ーーー mail, postal item
- 投函^{とうかん} ーーー mailing, posting
- 洋服屋^{ようふくや} ーーー *(western)* clothing store, tailor
- 軒^{けん} ーーー counter for buildings
- はしごする ーーー to bar hop, to go from and to
- 美容院^{びよういん} ーーー hair salon, beauty salon
- 余裕^{よゆう} ーーー time (to spare), room (to spare), leeway

第7章

- 合流(ごうりゅう) ーーー joining, merging, uniting
- 近況(きんきょう) ーーー current situation, recent state
- 報告(ほうこく) ーーー report, information
- 近況報告(きんきょうほうこく) ーーー catching up on what's going on
- 広場(ひろば) ーーー (public) square, plaza, open space
- コンサートを開(ひら)く ーーー to hold or play a concert
- 数曲(すうきょく) ーーー a few songs
- 遊園地(ゆうえんち) ーーー amusement park
- 閉鎖(へいさ) ーーー closing, shutdown, lockout
- 上映(じょうえい) ーーー showing (a movie), screening (a movie)
- 料理店(りょうりてん) ーーー restaurant
- 早(はや)めに ーーー earlier than usual, ahead of time, quickly
- 鳥肌(とりはだ)が立(た)つ ーーー to get goosebumps
- 味(あじ)わう ーーー to taste, to enjoy, to experience
- 満足(まんぞく) ーーー satisfaction, content, happy
- 更(ふ)け ーーー getting late, growing late
- 繁華街(はんかがい) ーーー downtown, shopping district
- 検索(けんさく) ーーー search, looking up
- 中世(ちゅうせい) ーーー the Middle Ages, medieval times
- 城(しろ) ーーー castle
- 旗(はた) ーーー flag, banner

- 鎧兜(よろいかぶと) ――― armor
- 玉座(ぎょくざ) ――― throne
- 飾(かざ)る ――― to decorate, to adorn, to display
- 弾(はず)み ――― bounce, momentum, spur of the moment
- 酔(よ)っぱらう ――― to get drunk
- 酔(よ)いを覚(さ)ます ――― to sober up
- 高(たか)くつく ――― to be costly, to be expensive
- そもそも ――― in the first place, to begin with, anyway
- 時間(じかん)をつぶす ――― to kill time
- 遊歩道(ゆうほどう) ――― promenade, boardwalk, walkway
- 寄(よ)る ――― to approach, to gather, to stop by
- 軽食(けいしょく) ――― snack, light meal
- 別(わか)れ ――― farewell, goodbye, parting
- 交(か)わす ――― to exchange, … each other, to cross
- 帰路(きろ)につく ――― to head home

第7章

読解問題(どっかいもんだい)

1. 銀行口座(ぎんこうこうざ)にお金(かね)を入(い)れることは何(なん)と言(い)いますか？

    A) 出金(しゅっきん)
    B) 残高確認(ざんだかかくにん)
    C) 口座開設(こうざかいせつ)
    D) 入金(にゅうきん)

2. マコトはショッピングモールで何(なに)をしていましたか？

    A) ゲームセンターでゲームをした
    B) 友達(ともだち)と遊(あそ)んだり、洋服(ようふく)を買(か)ったりした
    C) 洋服(ようふく)を買(か)って、髪(かみ)を切(き)った
    D) 髪(かみ)を切(き)って、フードコートで昼食(ちゅうしょく)をとった

3. 公園(こうえん)を出(で)てすぐ、二人(ふたり)はどこに向(む)かいましたか？

    A) 遊園地(ゆうえんち)
    B) 自宅(じたく)
    C) 映画館(えいがかん)
    D) レストラン

4. 二人(ふたり)はどうやって中世(ちゅうせい)をテーマにしたバーを知(し)ったのですか？

    A) バーを探(さが)して歩(ある)いていた
    B) 共通(きょうつう)の友人(ゆうじん)から勧(すす)められた
    C) スマートフォンで近(ちか)くのバーを検索(けんさく)した
    D) バーの広告(こうこく)を見(み)た

5. 酔っ払っている時にすると危険なことは次のうちどれですか？
   A) もっと飲む
   B) 自動車を運転する
   C) 電話をする
   D) 公共の場を歩き回る

English Translation

Before his big date with Sachiko that day, Makoto had a few errands to run. First of all, he had to go to the bank, so he could withdraw some cash. Along the way to the bank, he fueled up on caffeine from his favorite coffee shop to start the day.

 Next, he went to the post office and dropped off some overdue mail. After that, it was off to the mall to find new clothes to wear on his date. He had enough time to hit two clothing stores and get a haircut at the barber shop.

 At 2:00 pm, Makoto and Sachiko met up and decided to take a walk around the city. First, they strolled about the park while catching up with each other. Inside the park was a large plaza, where a rock band was giving a small concert. After hearing a few songs, the two left the park and drove to a local amusement park.

 The amusement park had apparently had a major accident and was closed, so the couple decided to go to the movie theater. Fortunately, it looked like a horror movie was playing that week. It would be an hour-long wait before the film was shown, so they grabbed an early dinner at a nearby Mexican restaurant and came back to the theater. The horror movie ended up being quite satisfying since it scared them enough to give them goosebumps.

 As the evening came, the couple felt they didn't want to stay out too late downtown, but they agreed to have one drink at a

第7章

unique bar they found searching on their smartphones. It was a bar with a medieval castle theme, decorated with banners, suits of armor, and throne-like chairs. The conversation picked up between the two and along with it came more drinking.

Now they were both drunk and were worrying about getting home. Not in the mood to go to a club, they would wait two hours to sober up before going home. Calling a taxi would be costly, and it wasn't all that much of a wait to begin with. To pass the time, they walked along the boardwalk and stopped by the convenience store for a snack.

Makoto and Sachiko enjoyed being together on their date, making the hours pass quicker than expected, but it was time to part ways. A brief kiss was shared, and then, they headed home.

第8章

日曜日の午後だった。マコトは特に予定もなかったので、昼間に寝て平日の睡眠不足を取り戻した。しかし一日中だらけている時間はない、溜まった家事をしなければならない。

中でも重要なのは未払いの請求書。生活はタダではできない。家賃、電気代、水道代、インターネット代、ローン、電話代などなど。コンビニに行けばすべて解決する。

次に1週間で溜まった洗濯物。次の週に必要なものを考えれば、1回、2回は回さなければいけない。白、黒、色と分けることなく、洗濯物を入れられるだけ入れて、洗剤と柔軟剤を入れて洗濯機を回した。

洗濯が終わるのを待っている間、皿洗いをしたり、掃除機をかけたりして休日をムダにしない。マコトの家は決してキレイな家とは言えなかったが、毎週少しずつできることをやっていた。今週は、キッチ

第8章

ンを少しきれいにしておこうと思い、冷蔵庫の中を掃除し、**賞味期限**切れの**食品**を**捨**てる。さらに、カウンターを**消毒**して**磨**き、**床**に**落**ちたゴミをブラシで**落**とし、**最後**に**ほうきとちりとり**で**床**を**掃**いた。モップ**がけ**は**来週**にしよう。

マコトは、**残**りの**時間**でテレビゲームをしようと思っていた。**特**に**戦略**ゲームが好きで、**一人用**のゲームやオンラインゲームで**友人**と**対戦**しながら、**何時間**もかけて**新**しい**戦略**を**考**えていた。**一息つき**たいときには、**軽**くストレッチをして**窓**の**外**を**眺**め、**電子**レンジで**食**べ**物**を**温**め、また**座**ってゲームをすることもある。

何時間もゲームをしていると、**ちょっとした疑問**が**訪**れた。**時間**をもっと**有意義**なことに使えるはず**のに**、ゲームに**費**やすのは**本当**に**賢明**なことなのだろうか？もちろん、ネットで**動画**を**見**ることもできるが、それは**違**うのだろうか？そう思い、**寝室**でヘッドホンを**手**に**取**り、サチコから**勧**められたオーディオブックを**聴**き**始**めた。

この本を聴いていると、これこそ正しい時間の使い方のように感じられ、自分を見つめ直す機会にもなった。本を聴きながら家の中をぶらぶらと歩いた。特に理由もなくクローゼットの扉を開けたり閉めたりした。歩きながらソファに手をかけ滑らせるように動かした。一人暮らしで、普段はキッチンかベランダで食事をしているので、この動作を繰り返すためのダイニングテーブルがないのだ。

気がつくともう夜の10時になっていた、寝る時間だ。オーディオブックはまだ聞き終えていないが、来週末にある親戚の集まりで、何か新しい話の種になるに違いない。サチコを連れて行って、この本を紹介してくれた人物として紹介することもできるだろう。

単語

- 昼間 ――― daytime, during the day
- 平日 ――― weekday, ordinary days
- 睡眠不足 ――― lack of sleep, sleep deprivation
- 取り戻す ――― to get back, to regain, to recover
- だらける ――― to be lazy, to slack off, to feel sluggish

第8章

- 家事(かじ) ーーー housework, chores
- 重要(じゅうよう) ーーー important
- 未払い(みはらい) ーーー unpaid
- 請求書(せいきゅうしょ) ーーー bill, invoice
- 家賃(やちん) ーーー rent
- 電気代(でんきだい) ーーー electric bill
- 水道代(すいどうだい) ーーー water bill
- ローン ーーー loan, lawn
- 解決(かいけつ) ーーー settlement, resolution, solution
- 洗濯物(せんたくもの) ーーー laundry, washing
- 回す(まわす) ーーー to turn (around/on), to send (around), to invest
- 分ける(わける) ーーー to divide (into), to separate, to split
- 洗剤(せんざい) ーーー detergent, cleanser
- 柔軟剤(じゅうなんざい) ーーー fabric softener
- 洗濯機(せんたくき) ーーー washing machine
- 皿洗い(さらあらい) ーーー doing the dishes
- 掃除機(そうじき) ーーー vacuum (cleaner)
- 休日(きゅうじつ) ーーー holiday, day off
- 無駄にしない(むだにしない) ーーー make the most of, make good use of
- 少しずつ(すこしずつ) ーーー little by little
- ずつ ーーー apiece, each, at a time

- 賞味期限(しょうみきげん) ――― expiration date, shelf life
- ～切れ(ぎ) ――― running out of..., completely using up...
- 賞味期限切れ(しょうみきげんぎ) ――― expired
- 食品(しょくひん) ――― food (products)
- 消毒(しょうどく) ――― disinfectant, sterilization
- 床(ゆか) ――― floor
- 箒(ほうき) *(usually written in just kana)* ――― broom
- ちりとり ――― dustpan
- 掃く(は) ――― to sweep, to brush
- モップがけ ――― mopping
- 残り(のこ) ――― remaining, remainder, leftover
- 戦略(せんりゃく) ――― strategy
- 一人用(ひとりよう) ――― (for) one person
- 対戦(たいせん) ――― match, fight, game
- 一息つく(ひといき) ――― to take a break, to take a breath
- 眺める(なが) ――― to look, to stare at, to view
- 電子レンジ(でんし) ――― microwave (oven)
- 温める(あたた) ――― to warm (up), to heat (up), to mull over *(an idea)*
- ちょっとした ――― small, slight, bit of a
- 訪れる(おとず) ――― to visit, to come
- 有意義(ゆういぎ) ――― meaningful, significant, valuable

第8章

- のに ーーー (al)though, if only, in order to
- 費(つい)やす ーーー to spend, to devote, to waste
- 寝室(しんしつ) ーーー bedroom
- 勧(すす)める ーーー to recommend, to advise, to offer
- こそ ーーー used to emphasize the preceding word
- 見(み)つめ直(なお)す ーーー to reconsider, to take another good look at
- ぶらぶら ーーー dangling, wandering, aimlessly
- 扉(とびら) ーーー door, gate, title page
- 手(て)をかける ーーー to lay hands on, to have a hand on
- 滑(すべ)る ーーー to glide or slide, to ski or skate, to slip
- 一人暮(ひとりぐ)らし ーーー living alone
- 普段(ふだん) ーーー usual(ly), normal(ly), everyday
- 動作(どうさ) ーーー movement, action, operation *(of a machine)*
- 繰(く)り返(かえ)す ーーー to repeat
- 親戚(しんせき) ーーー relative, family
- 集(あつ)まり ーーー gathering, meeting, collection
- 話(はなし)の種(たね) ーーー topic of conversation
- 違(ちが)いない ーーー one is sure that, no doubt that, for certain
- 連(つ)れて行(い)く ーーー to take someone to some place

読解問題(どっかいもんだい)

1. 睡眠不足(すいみんぶそく)を解消(かいしょう)する必要(ひつよう)がある時(とき)はどんな時(とき)ですか？

    A) 寝(ね)すぎ
    B) 睡眠時間(すいみんじかん)が短(みじか)すぎる
    C) 睡眠(すいみん)を楽(たの)しんでいる
    D) 寝落(ねお)ちに苦労(くろう)している

2. 次(つぎ)のうち、生活費(せいかつひ)とみなされないものはどれですか？

    A) ローン
    B) 水道(すいどう)
    C) 電気(でんき)
    D) インターネット

3. キッチンを掃除(そうじ)するときにマコトがしなかったことは次(つぎ)のうちどれですか？

    A) カウンターを消毒(しょうどく)してこすり洗(あら)い
    B) 賞味期限切(しょうみきげんぎ)れの食品(しょくひん)を捨(す)てる
    C) 床(ゆか)のモップ掛(が)け
    D) ほうきとちりとりで床(ゆか)を掃(は)く

第8章

4. 一般に食べ物を最も早く調理する方法は次のうちどれですか？

   A) コンロ

   B) 電子レンジ

   C) オーブン

   D) トースター

5. マコトはヘッドホンをどこで見つけましたか？

   A) 寝室

   B) クローゼット

   C) 洗濯機

   D) リビング

English Translation

It was a Sunday afternoon. Makoto had no particular plans, so he slept in to catch up on sleep he had missed during the week. There was no time to slack off all day though, for he had to do a number of household chores.

Most important of all were the unpaid bills. Life doesn't come for free. This includes rent, electricity, water, internet, loans, phone plans, and so on. All of these can be resolved by going to the convenience store.

Next was the laundry that had piled up over the week. Thinking about clothes needed for the next week, running one or two loads would be necessary. Without sorting his laundry into whites, darks, and colors, he would just throw in as much as he could, add laundry detergent and fabric softener, and run the laundry machine.

While he waited for the laundry to finish, he did the dishes and vacuumed the house to make the best use of his day off. Makoto's house was by no means spotless, but he did just a little bit each week to maintain what he could. This week, he thought to do some extra work in the kitchen, so he cleaned out the fridge and threw away expired foods. He also disinfected and scrubbed down the counters, brushing off any debris to the ground, and finally, swept the floor with his broom and dustpan. He'll do the mopping next week, he thought.

For the remainder of his time, Makoto wanted to play video games. He was particularly fond of strategy games, and would spend hours thinking about new strategies to try out in single player and against his friends online. When he needed a break, he would do some light stretching, gaze out the windows, heat up some food in the microwave, and sit back down for more gaming.

After spending too many hours playing, a question came up. Was it really all that wise to spend so much time gaming when it could be used for something more meaningful? Sure, there were videos he could watch on the internet, but would that be any different? With that in mind, he picked up the headphones in his bedroom and started to listen to some of the audiobook recommended to him by Sachiko.

Listening to the book instantly felt like the right use of his time and even opened up the opportunity for some self-reflection. While listening to the book, he wandered around his house. He opened and closed his closet doors for no particular reason. He put his hand on the sofa and let it glide over as he walked across. There was no dining room table to repeat this action, as he lived alone and usually ate in the kitchen or out on the balcony.

Before he knew it, it was 10:00 pm, and it was time for bed. While he didn't finish the audiobook, he certainly had something new to talk about next weekend when he would go to the family

第8章

gathering. He could even bring Sachiko and introduce her as the one who introduced him to the book.

第9章

サチコは、翌週末に行われるマコトの親族との集まりに同行することを快く承諾してくれた。これで正式なカップルになったわけだし、母や父、兄弟に彼女を紹介するいい機会になりそうだ。

集まりには、マコトの叔父であるイサムも来ていた。彼は、蒸気タービン、ガスタービン、発電機など、あらゆる機械を扱う機械技師だ。非常に頭のいい人で、若いころマコトにいろいろなことを教えてくれた人でもある。

叔父と話をしていると、後ろに従兄弟のケンジとユウコがいることに気がついた。この3人は、子供の頃からよく遊び、色々なことを一緒にしてきた。しかし、大人になるにつれて疎遠になり、社会人になってからは音信不通になってしまっていたのだ。ケンジは小売店の管理

第9章

職にまで上り詰め、ユウコはパートタイムの美容師をしながら主婦になっていた。

サチコは初対面の人たちに圧倒されていたが、ある人物と仲良くなれた。マコトの義理の妹のノリコである。二人は最初から意気投合し、すぐに打ち解けることができた。サチコはジャーナリストであり、ノリコは勤めている会社が制作しているテレビ番組の脚本家だったのだ。会社で顔を合わせることはあっても、今まで一度も面と向かって会ったことはなかったらしい。

結局、サチコは全員に挨拶することはできず、マコトにとっても追いつけないほど多くの人がいた。祖母や叔母には軽く挨拶したが、姪や甥には挨拶できなかった。子供たちは皆、別室で遊ぶのに夢中だ。

最後にサチコも誘って家族で集合写真を撮った。毎年、家族写真の担当をしているのはマコトの父親である。プロの写真家である父に任せるのは、理にかなっている。

日が暮れ始め、次第にお開きの雰囲気になっている。みんなが帰路につく中、マコトはもう一度イサムと話をすることにした。今の保険会社での仕事に限界を感じ、いくつかの進路を考えているという相談をするためだ。イサムは、「どこに転職するにせよ、できるだけ早く何かしら勉強し始めた方がいい」というアドバイスを送った。このまま待っているだけなのは一番よくない。

単語

- 翌週末 ーーー next weekend, the following weekend
- 同行 ーーー accompanying, traveling together
- 快く ーーー willingly, pleasantly, gladly
- 承諾 ーーー consent, approval, acceptance
- 正式 ーーー formal, official
- わけだ ーーー it makes sense that..., that explains..., no wonder
- 蒸気タービン ーーー steam turbine
- 発電機 ーーー (electric) generator
- あらゆる ーーー every, all
- 扱う ーーー to handle, to deal with, to operate
- 機械技師 ーーー mechanical engineer

第9章

- 若(わか)いころ −−− (one's) youth, when one was young
- でもある −−− to also be *(formal, literary)*
- 従兄弟(いとこ) −−− *(male)* cousin
- 子供(こども)の頃(ころ) −−− one's childhood, when one was a child
- 疎遠(そえん)になる −−− to grow apart, to lose touch, to lose contact
- 音信不通(おんしんふつう) −−− not hearing from, can't reach, lost contact with
- 小売店(こうりてん) −−− retail store, retailer
- 管理職(かんりしょく) −−− management, manager, administrative position
- 上(のぼ)り詰(つ)め −−− to climb to the top, to reach the top
- 美容師(びようし) −−− hairdresser, hair stylist, barber
- 主婦(しゅふ) −−− housewife
- 初対面(しょたいめん) −−− first time meeting
- 圧倒(あっとう) −−− overwhelming
- 義理(ぎり)の妹(いもうと) −−− sister-in-law
- 意気投合(いきとうごう) −−− hit it off, clicking (with another person)
- 打(う)ち解(と)ける −−− to open up to a person
- 勤(つと)める −−− to work (at/for/in), to serve (as)
- 制作(せいさく) −−− production, work (of art)
- 番組(ばんぐみ) −−− (TV) program
- 脚本家(きゃくほんか) −−− screenwriter, scriptwriter, playwright
- 顔(かお)を合(あ)わせる −−− to meet, to face someone

- 面(めん)と向(む)かう ――― to meet face-to-face
- 結局(けっきょく) ――― after all, in the end, eventually
- 追(お)いつく ――― to catch up (with/to), to keep up (with)
- 祖母(そぼ) ――― grandmother
- 叔母(おば) ――― aunt
- 姪(めい) ――― niece
- 甥(おい) ――― nephew
- 別室(べっしつ) ――― another room, separate room
- 夢中(むちゅう) ――― absorbed in, immersed in, obsessed with
- 集合写真(しゅうごうしゃしん) ――― group photo
- 担当(たんとう) ――― in charge of
- 父親(ちちおや) ――― father
- 写真家(しゃしんか) ――― photographer
- 任(まか)せる ――― to leave to, to entrust, to let
- 理(り)にかなう ――― to make sense
- 日(ひ)が暮(く)れる ――― to set (*e.g. the sun*)
- 次第(しだい)に ――― gradually
- お開(ひら)き ――― coming to a close, calling it a night
- 雰囲気(ふんいき) ――― (an) atmosphere, (a certain) air, vibe
- 進路(しんろ) ――― (future) course, path, route
- 相談(そうだん) ――― asking for advice, consultation, discussion

第9章

- <ruby>転職<rt>てんしょく</rt></ruby> ーーー job change, career change
- にせよ ーーー even if, whether...or, whatever
- できるだけ<ruby>早<rt>はや</rt></ruby>く ーーー as soon as possible
- このまま ーーー like this, as is, as things are

<ruby>読解問題<rt>どっかい もんだい</rt></ruby>

1. マコトの<ruby>叔父<rt>おじ</rt></ruby>の<ruby>職業<rt>しょくぎょう</rt></ruby>は<ruby>何<rt>なん</rt></ruby>ですか？
    A) <ruby>電気技師<rt>でんきぎし</rt></ruby>
    B) <ruby>土木技師<rt>どぼくぎし</rt></ruby>
    C) <ruby>化学技師<rt>かがくぎし</rt></ruby>
    D) <ruby>機械技師<rt>きかいぎし</rt></ruby>

2. ケンジとユウコの<ruby>両親<rt>りょうしん</rt></ruby>は、マコトにとって<ruby>次<rt>つぎ</rt></ruby>のうちどれに<ruby>当<rt>あ</rt></ruby>てはまりますか？
    A) <ruby>祖父<rt>そふ</rt></ruby>と<ruby>祖母<rt>そぼ</rt></ruby>
    B) <ruby>母<rt>はは</rt></ruby>と<ruby>父<rt>ちち</rt></ruby>
    C) <ruby>叔母<rt>おば</rt></ruby>と<ruby>叔父<rt>おじ</rt></ruby>
    D) <ruby>兄妹<rt>けいまい</rt></ruby>

3. マコトにとって義理の姉は誰と結婚していますか？
    A) 兄
    B) 父
    C) いとこ
    D) 上司

4. 家族が集まっている間、子供たちはどこで遊んでいましたか？
    A) 学校
    B) 家の中
    C) 別室
    D) おもちゃ部屋

5. 仕事に必要な高い能力を持っている人は次のうち何と呼ばれますか？
    A) 素人
    B) 労働者
    C) 職業
    D) プロ

第9章

English Translation

Sachiko happily agreed to accompany Makoto on his visit to his family gathering the following weekend. They were now officially a couple, and it would be a good time to introduce her to his mother, father, and brothers.

Also at the get-together was Makoto's uncle, named Isamu. Isamu was a mechanical engineer who handled all kinds of machines, including steam and gas turbines and electric generators. He was an extremely intelligent person who taught Makoto many things in his younger years.

While talking with his uncle, he noticed his two cousins Kenji and Yuko in the background. The three of them hung out quite frequently and did many things together as kids. They grew apart as they grew up, however, and lost contact with one another as they entered the workforce. Kenji ended up working his way up to a management position at a retail store, and Yuko was a housewife and worked as a part-time hairdresser.

Sachiko was obviously overwhelmed by all the new faces, but she did make friends with someone. This person was Makoto's sister-in-law Noriko. From the very start, the two hit it off and warmed up to each other. Sachiko was a journalist, and Noriko was a writer for a TV show that was produced by the same company they both worked for. While they had seen each other around the office, they had seemingly never met face-to-face until now.

In the end, Sachiko couldn't meet and greet everyone, and there were too many people for Makoto to catch up with. They briefly said hello to his grandmother and aunts, but they never got to greet his nieces and nephews. All the kids were busy playing in a separate room.

At the end of the day, the family took *(lit. was able to take)* a group photo, which included Sachiko, who was invited to join in. Every year, it was Makoto's dad who was in charge of the family photo. Leaving the task to him made sense, given that he was a professional photographer.

The sun was beginning to set, and the event was gradually coming to a close. As everyone was heading home, Makoto decided to speak with Uncle Isamu once again. He told him that he felt he was burning out at his current job at the insurance company and was considering several career paths he could take. Uncle Isamu advised him that, no matter what job he changes to, he should start studying something as soon as possible. Just waiting around was the worst thing he could do.

第10章

フルタイムの仕事もあり、彼女もいる、タイトなスケジュールでマコトは日々を過ごしていた。しかし、より良い未来のために、地元の大学で経済学を学ぶために大学院に入学した。

すでに学部課程を卒業し、哲学の学士号を取得していたが、入学が決まれば過去に勉強していたことなんて関係ない。なんせマコトの大学生活というのは、終身雇用制の社会人になるまでの自由を謳歌する猶予期間でしかなかったのだ。

しかし、今回は違う。経験も知恵も豊富なこのチャンスを無駄にはできない。大学院で経済学を学ぶのは大変な挑戦だが、成功すれば大きな報酬を得ることができる。学部時代の授業は、これに比べれば楽なものだった。入試の時と同じように、またもや猛勉強と根性が必要となる。

講義よりも、教科書の方がよほど役に立つことが多い。先生によっては、授業中に集中力を持続させるのが難しいほどである。長話をする教授もいた。教科書を読むのに半分の時間を費やすだけで、講義で得た情報の2倍を得ることができた。

情報を定着させるためには、学校外で真剣に取り組むことが必要不可欠だ。学生たちが組織した勉強会は、マコトが授業で成果をあげるために必要なモチベーションと意欲を与えてくれた。授業で取ったノートを共有し、試験に出そうなところを共に復習する。しかし、猛勉強するだけではなく、休憩時間には雑談をして溜まったストレスやフラストレーションを発散することもあった。

1年次の期末テストが近づき、直近数回の講義では教室が不安に包まれていた。テストは小論文形式で、選択式ではない。詰め込み勉強は通用しないのだ。良い成績を取るためには、情報を網羅して知っていなければならない。マコトをはじめ、クラスメートは高額な授業料を払っているが、全員が試験を通過できるわけではない。講義

第10章

を受け、勉強会に参加し、本をたくさん読んだ者が突破できるのである。

正に外国語の勉強のように、その外国語にどっぷり浸かった者が成功する仕組みだ。その言語でできるだけ多くの文章を読み、読めなくなったら、自由な時間は言語を聞くことに費やす。今までの趣味や生活スタイルよりも優先しなければ成功はできない。その積み重ねで高いレベルの流暢さというものは獲得できるのだ。

問題は、マコトが期末試験に合格したかどうかではなく、流暢に話せるようになるために必要なことをするかどうかということに尽きる。

勉強頑張ってください、そして読んでくださってありがとうございました！

単語

- 地元 ーーー local, hometown, local area
- 経済学 ーーー economics
- 大学院 ーーー graduate school

Japanese Short Stories for Intermediate Learners

- 入学（にゅうがく） --- admission *(to a school)*, enrollment
- 学部課程（がくぶかてい） --- undergraduate course
- 卒業（そつぎょう） --- graduation, outgrowing something
- 哲学（てつがく） --- philosophy
- 学士号（がくしごう） --- bachelor's degree
- 取得（しゅとく） --- acquisition, obtaining, getting
- なんて --- used to emphasize a feeling, what, things like
- 関係ない（かんけいない） --- has nothing to do with, doesn't matter, unrelated
- なにせ／なんせ --- at any rate, because, anyhow
- 終身雇用制（しゅうしんこようせい） --- (Japanese) lifetime employment system
- 自由（じゆう） --- free, freedom, liberty
- 謳歌（おうか） --- enjoying, rejoicing, singing praises
- 猶予期間（ゆうよきかん） --- grace period
- 知恵（ちえ） --- wisdom, intelligence, wit
- 豊富（ほうふ） --- rich, abundant, abundance
- 報酬（ほうしゅう） --- reward, compensation
- 得る（える） --- to get, to obtain, to be able to
- 学部時代（がくぶじだい） --- one's undergraduate days
- 入試（にゅうし） --- entrance exam
- またもや --- (once) again
- 猛勉強（もうべんきょう） --- intense studying

第10章

- <ruby>根性<rt>こんじょう</rt></ruby> ーーー willpower, guts, (one's) nature
- <ruby>講義<rt>こうぎ</rt></ruby> ーーー lecture
- <ruby>教科書<rt>きょうかしょ</rt></ruby> ーーー textbook
- よほど ーーー very, much, almost
- によって ーーー by (means of), because of
- <ruby>集中力<rt>しゅうちゅうりょく</rt></ruby> ーーー (power of) concentration, ability to focus
- <ruby>持続<rt>じぞく</rt></ruby> ーーー continuation, continuance
- <ruby>教授<rt>きょうじゅ</rt></ruby> ーーー professor, teaching
- <ruby>定着<rt>ていちゃく</rt></ruby> ーーー staying *(to one place)*, fixing, taking root
- <ruby>学校外<rt>がっこうがい</rt></ruby> ーーー outside of school
- <ruby>真剣<rt>しんけん</rt></ruby> ーーー serious, real sword *(as opposed to a wooded one)*
- <ruby>取り組む<rt>とく</rt></ruby> ーーー to wrestle with, to be matched against, to tackle
- <ruby>必要不可欠<rt>ひつようふかけつ</rt></ruby> ーーー (absolutely) essential, indispensable, crucial
- <ruby>組織<rt>そしき</rt></ruby> ーーー (an) organization, structure, tissue *(biology)*
- <ruby>勉強会<rt>べんきょうかい</rt></ruby> ーーー study group
- <ruby>成果<rt>せいか</rt></ruby>をあげる ーーー to produce results, to get good results
- <ruby>意欲<rt>いよく</rt></ruby> ーーー will, desire, eagerness
- <ruby>共有<rt>きょうゆう</rt></ruby> ーーー joint ownership, sharing
- <ruby>雑談<rt>ざつだん</rt></ruby> ーーー chatting, light conversation
- <ruby>発散<rt>はっさん</rt></ruby> ーーー emission, venting, divergence
- <ruby>年次<rt>ねんじ</rt></ruby> ーーー annual, yearly, nth year

- 期末テスト（きまつテスト）――― final exam, end of term test
- 直近数回（ちょっきんすうかい）――― the last few times
- 包む（つつむ）――― to wrap (up), to cover, to conceal
- 小論文形式（しょうろんぶんけいしき）――― essay format
- 選択式（せんたくしき）――― multiple choice
- 詰め込み勉強（つめこみべんきょう）――― cramming (for a test)
- 通用しない（つうようしない）――― doesn't work, doesn't cut it
- 成績（せいせき）――― grades, results
- 網羅（もうら）――― including all, covering all
- 高額（こうがく）――― large amount (of money)
- 授業料（じゅぎょうりょう）――― tuition (fees)
- 通過（つうか）――― passing (through), transit
- わけではない ――― it doesn't mean that, it's not like
- 突破（とっぱ）――― breaking through, overcoming, exceeding
- 正に（まさに）――― exactly, just, indeed
- どっぷり浸かる（どっぷりつかる）――― to be completely immersed
- 仕組み（しくみ）――― mechanism, system, structure
- 文章（ぶんしょう）――― writing, written work, sentence
- 優先（ゆうせん）――― priority, precedence, preference
- 積み重ね（つみかさね）――― pile, accumulation
- 流暢（りゅうちょう）――― fluent

第10章

- <ruby>獲得<rt>かくとく</rt></ruby> ーーー acquisition
- <ruby>合格<rt>ごうかく</rt></ruby> ーーー passing (a test/an inspection), meeting standards
- <ruby>尽<rt>つ</rt></ruby>きる ーーー to run out, to be used up

<ruby>読解問題<rt>どっかい もんだい</rt></ruby>

1. マコトはどこで<ruby>経済<rt>けいざい</rt></ruby>の<ruby>授業<rt>じゅぎょう</rt></ruby>を<ruby>受<rt>う</rt></ruby>けていましたか？

    A) オンラインコース
    B) <ruby>地元<rt>じもと</rt></ruby>の<ruby>大学<rt>だいがく</rt></ruby>
    C) <ruby>短大<rt>たんだい</rt></ruby>
    D) <ruby>家庭教師<rt>かていきょうし</rt></ruby>

2. <ruby>挑戦<rt>ちょうせん</rt></ruby>が<ruby>大変<rt>たいへん</rt></ruby>であるということは、<ruby>次<rt>つぎ</rt></ruby>のうちどれを<ruby>表<rt>あらわ</rt></ruby>していますか？

    A) <ruby>簡単<rt>かんたん</rt></ruby>
    B) <ruby>不可能<rt>ふかのう</rt></ruby>
    C) <ruby>手<rt>て</rt></ruby>ごわい
    D) <ruby>可能<rt>かのう</rt></ruby>

3. <ruby>講義<rt>こうぎ</rt></ruby>の<ruby>問題点<rt>もんだいてん</rt></ruby>は<ruby>何<rt>なん</rt></ruby>でしたか？

    A) <ruby>授業<rt>じゅぎょう</rt></ruby>が<ruby>夜遅<rt>よるおそ</rt></ruby>くまで<ruby>行<rt>おこな</rt></ruby>われていた
    B) マコトの<ruby>友達<rt>ともだち</rt></ruby>が<ruby>授業中<rt>じゅぎょうちゅう</rt></ruby>にしゃべっていた
    C) <ruby>教授<rt>きょうじゅ</rt></ruby>の<ruby>説明<rt>せつめい</rt></ruby>が<ruby>複雑<rt>ふくざつ</rt></ruby>すぎた
    D) <ruby>教授<rt>きょうじゅ</rt></ruby>が<ruby>生徒<rt>せいと</rt></ruby>を<ruby>嫌<rt>きら</rt></ruby>っていた

4. 勉強会を組織したのは誰でしたか？
    A) 生徒たち
    B) 大学
    C) マコト
    D) 教授

5. 期末テストはどのようなテストでしたか？
    A) すべて選択式
    B) 選択問題と論述問題が混在した問題
    C) 詰め込みと高額な授業料のミックス
    D) 小論文問題のみ

English Translation

With a full-time job and a girlfriend, Makoto was on a tight schedule. But for the sake of a better future, he enrolled in a graduate school to study economics at a local university.

Makoto had already completed an undergraduate program and graduated with a bachelor's degree in philosophy, yet it really didn't matter what he studied back then after getting accepted. The university life of Makoto was only a grace period to enjoy freedom until he became a working adult in the Japanese system of lifetime employment.

But this time would be different. With much more experience and wisdom, this opportunity would not go wasted. Studying economics in graduate school was going to be a serious challenge, but if he succeeded, the rewards would be great. The classes he took as an undergraduate would be a cakewalk compared to this. Intense

第10章

study and perseverance would once again be required just like the college entrance exam.

The textbooks were often much more useful than the lectures. Some of the professors made it difficult to maintain focus in class. Some simply talked for too long. He could spend half the time reading chapters from the book and get double the information he got in the lecture hall.

To make the information stick, it was essential to do serious work outside the classroom. Study groups organized by students provided Makoto the motivation and desire needed to do well in the course. The students shared the notes they took in class and reviewed the information together they thought would be on the exams. Studying hard was not everything though, as they also took breaks to chat and vent built-up stress and frustration.

Finals for the first year were approaching, and anxiety filled the classroom during the last few lectures. The test would be essay questions only; there would be no multiple choice. Cramming wasn't going to get you anywhere. You had to know the information in and out in order to get a good grade. Makoto and his classmates paid high tuition fees, but not all would pass the test. It would be those who attended the lectures, participated in the study groups, and read a lot that would pass.

It was very much like learning a foreign language; those who succeed are those who immerse themselves in the foreign language. They read as much text as possible in that language, and when they can no longer read, they spend their free time listening to the language. Success cannot happen without immersion taking precedence over their old hobbies and lifestyles. That's how they are able to acquire high levels of fluency.

The question is not whether or not Makoto passed the final exam but whether or not you will do what it takes in order to become fluent.

Study hard, and thank you for reading!

ABOUT THE AUTHOR

Language Guru is a brand created by a hardcore language enthusiast with a passion for creating simple but great products. They work with a large team of native speakers from across the world to make sure each product is the absolute best quality it can be.

Each product and new edition represents the opportunity to surpass themselves and previous works. The key to achieving this has always been to work from the perspective of the learner.

DID YOU ENJOY THE READ?

Thank you so much for taking the time to read our book! We hope you have enjoyed it and learned tons of vocabulary in the process.

If you would like to support our work, please consider writing a customer review on Amazon. It would mean the world to us!

We read each and every single review posted, and we use all the feedback we receive to write even better books.

ANSWER KEY

Chapter 1:
1) D
2) B
3) B
4) B
5) A

Chapter 2:
1) C
2) D
3) B
4) C
5) C

Chapter 3:
1) B
2) C
3) A
4) D
5) B

Chapter 4:
1) D
2) B
3) A
4) C
5) C

Chapter 5:
1) D
2) C
3) A
4) D
5) B

Chapter 6:
1) D
2) B
3) B
4) A
5) C

Chapter 7:
1) D
2) C
3) A
4) C
5) B

Chapter 8:
1) B
2) A
3) C
4) B
5) A

Chapter 9:
1) D
2) C
3) A
4) C
5) D

Chapter 10:
1) B
2) C
3) C
4) A
5) D

www.ingramcontent.com/pod-product-compliance
Lightning Source LLC
Chambersburg PA
CBHW022010120526
44592CB00034B/766